THE FUTURE OF THE RESEARCH LIBRARY

. . . .

Phineas L. Windsor Series in Librarianship

The Future of the Research Library

Verner W. Clapp

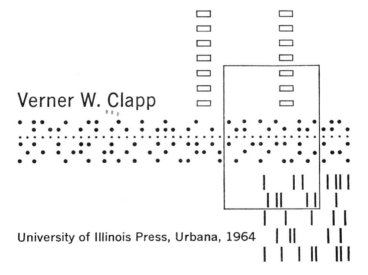

University of Illinois Press, Urbana, 1964

Foreword

· · · · · · · · · · · · · · · · · · · ·

The first of the Windsor Lectures in Librarianship were presented fifteen years ago by a well-known bookman, John T. Winterich. Since their inauguration in 1949, the lectures have become one of the most distinguished series in the country relating to books and libraries. The speaker for 1963, Verner W. Clapp, is the eighteenth to participate in the program. A variety of talents has been drawn upon from literary, academic, publishing, library, and other fields. All the lectures to date have been issued in handsome and appropriate formats by the University of Illinois Press, and several have approached the status of best sellers.

The professional contributions of the man in whose honor the lectureship is named are outstanding. When Phineas Lawrence Windsor retired in 1940, he had rounded out a notable career of more than forty years in librarianship, the last thirty-one of which were spent as director of the Library and Library School of the University of Illinois. Under Professor Windsor's guidance, the Library School became internationally known

vi   THE FUTURE OF THE RESEARCH LIBRARY

as one of the leading centers for professional education.
During the same period, the Library gained a position in
the forefront of American university libraries. The endowed lectureship, created by several thousand alumni
at the time of Professor Windsor's retirement, is both a
recognition of his longtime leadership in the library world
and fitting testimony of their loyalty, affection, and high
esteem for him.

Verner W. Clapp, Windsor lecturer for 1963, is emi-
nently qualified to deal with the theme "The Future of
the Research Library." He joined the Library of Congress staff when Herbert Putnam was a relatively young
man, and Dr. Putnam lived to be ninety-four. The comparison should not be pushed too far, however, for Mr.
Clapp was just out of Trinity College, Hartford, when
he went to Washington, in 1922. In the ensuing years,
he worked his way up through the Library of Congress
hierarchy until 1947, when he became Chief Assistant
Librarian. He and Luther Evans formed one of the most
remarkable teams ever to direct our national library, and
its prestige and influence under their leadership rose to
an all-time high, nationally and internationally. During
that period, Mr. Clapp found time for such related assignments as serving as librarian of the United Nations
Conference on International Organization in San Fran-
cisco in 1945, and as chairman of the United States
library mission to Japan in 1947-48.

Having been with the Library of Congress for thirty-
four years, it was taken for granted that Mr. Clapp was
a permanent fixture and would round out his career in
that famous institution. But then, in 1956, the Ford

Foundation granted $5,000,000 for establishment of the Council on Library Resources, for a five-year period, and persuaded Mr. Clapp to become its president. The Foundation showed satisfaction and further confidence in its choice in 1961 by an additional grant of $8,000,000 for an indeterminate period.

The purpose of the Council on Library Resources is to initiate and coordinate developments that will improve the extent and use of library resources and services. It tries, in Mr. Clapp's words, "to identify the problems which now present obstacles to efficient library service and to find methods for overcoming these impediments through new procedures and the applications of technological developments." Since its establishment seven years ago, the Council has operated in diverse areas, by way of numerous grants, to further these objectives. The Council's activities, under Mr. Clapp's direction, are doing much to shape the future research library.

> ROBERT B. DOWNS
> Dean of Library Administration
> University of Illinois

Contents

. . . .

|

· ·

"Gateways
to the World's Treasury
of Recorded Knowledge"

As World War II drew to a close, Fremont Rider, at that time the librarian of Wesleyan University, threw a bombshell into the library world by his demonstration of the exponential growth of research library collections. These, he found, had been doubling in size, on the average, every sixteen years. Projecting this rate of growth into the future, he calculated that the library of Yale University would by the year 2040 contain some 200 million volumes, while its catalog alone would occupy eight acres of floor space.

But Rider, ever a constructive critic, provided along with his prophecy of doom a gospel of salvation: the research library of the future, he foresaw, would consist of microtext; and not of microtext merely, but of microtext in a form in which the collections would serve as their own catalog.[1] Microcards, which he there and

. . . .
[1] F. Rider, *The Scholar and the Future of the Research Library* (New York: Hadham Press, 1944).

then invented, have since greatly contributed to the development of library resources, but they have not solved the problem of the exponential increase of library collections as their inventor hoped they would.

The reverberations of *The Scholar and the Future of the Research Library* have been echoing in a rising crescendo ever since. Twenty years later we are still discovering further and further evidences of the law of exponential growth in the affairs of libraries. In the very second of these Windsor Lectures, Dean Ridenour dwelt informatively and at length on this topic,[2] and even within the past few months we have seen at least two books expanding upon this theme.[3]

But it is the main topic of Rider's book — the means by which the threat to the research library might be averted — that has most held our attention since. The sounds of the war had not yet died away when a leading physicist, Dr. Vannevar Bush, gave rein to his imagination in a popular article on the manner in which the scholar of the future might assemble, organize, and recall the information necessary for his studies.[4] Few have noted, I think, that in the very month in which this article appeared, its author, as the director of the wartime Office of Scientific Research and Development,

. . . .

[2] L. N. Ridenour and others, *Bibliography in an Age of Science* (Urbana: University of Illinois Press, 1951), pp. 6-13, 30-35.

[3] D. J. de S. Price, *Science Since Babylon* (New Haven: Yale University Press, 1961); *Little Science, Big Science* (New York: Columbia University Press, 1963).

[4] V. Bush, "As We May Think," *Atlantic Monthly* 176:101-108 (July, 1945).

addressed a report to the President of the United States in which the same subject was discussed, not in terms of imaginative speculation, but of recommended governmental action.[5] It was, perhaps not unnaturally, the imaginative article that stimulated the most immediate response.

Certainly the meetings, articles, and reports that since the end of the war have been concerned with the future of the research library make a very lengthy list. It includes the second Windsor Lecture, to which I have already referred, in which two physicists and a librarian discussed *Bibliography in an Age of Science*. It includes, thirteen years later, and within the past month, the American Library Association's report to the Air Force on *The Library and Information Networks of the Future*.[6]

Under these circumstances, there seems to be little need to add to the speculation. I am a librarian, not an engineer; I make no pretense at competence in prognosticating the future capabilities of scientific and engineering developments as related to library work. Anyone who has worked with any of these — even with the simplest of them — has discovered the complexities which attend their introduction — complexities which are not only technological but procedural, economic, and sociological as well. Accordingly, I am very reluctant

. . . .

[5] V. Bush, *Science, the Endless Frontier* (Washington, D.C.: Government Printing Office, 1945).

[6] American Library Association, *The Library and Information Networks of the Future. Prepared for Rome Air Development Center, Air Force Systems Command . . . Griffis Air Force Base, New York* (Chicago: American Library Association, 1963).

once more to peer into the crystal ball and describe the role which it may be supposed that electronic devices and communication systems will play in libraries in the years to come.

Nevertheless, I admit to a certain responsibility here. As an officer of an organization whose charter it is to seek solutions to the problems of libraries generally and of research libraries in particular, I may be supposed to have some notions as to what these problems are, what kinds of solutions may be brought to them, and what the results may look like. Let me then turn to some of these.

LOCAL SELF-SUFFICIENCY *vs.* SHARING OF RESOURCES

From earliest times two principles have controlled the growth of libraries — the principle of local self-sufficiency and the principle of sharing the resources. The first of these demands that all materials needed for research be immediately at hand; the second, acknowledging the unattainability of the first, seeks methods to substitute for it. These principles have complemented each other throughout history. Each has been fortified from time to time by some development in technology, communication, or human relations; neither has ever won exclusive control and the likelihood is that neither ever will.

In the days of the earliest great libraries, a major effort seems to have been made to comply with the principle of local self-sufficiency. The number of books was still comparatively small, and the interest of scholars in books outside of their cultural areas was still undeveloped. The imperial libraries at Nineveh and Alexandria could, in consequence, with the use of the imperial treasury and the imperial authority, hope by purchase or compulsion to acquire a copy of every needed work, and even to translate into the official language of the empire the books of peoples incorporated into it (as in the case of Babylonian records at Nineveh and of the Septuagint at Alexandria).

It would be interesting to explore whether the principle of sharing of resources was ever applied in those early days. Did Nineveh or Alexandria possess catalogs of books held elsewhere? Were books ever borrowed from distant places without the intention of either commandeering or copying them? Whatever the answer, one can be fairly certain that in an area noted for its world travelers and its development of communications, there were undoubtedly scholars who, for example, found themselves unable to endure the Alexandrine summer and found it absolutely necessary to consult the texts in Pergamum.

In any case, these early comprehensive libraries perished. When comprehensiveness again became an ambition of libraries, several things had happened. Printing had been invented. This important technological development immediately gave enormous support to the principle of local self-sufficiency: many libraries might now acquire quickly and inexpensively what previously was obtainable only at great cost of time and effort. But printing had also so accelerated the deluge of bookmaking (of which mankind had already been complaining since before the Christian era) as to make the ambition of self-sufficiency even less attainable, if possible, than it had been earlier.

In our own days we have witnessed a technological contribution to the support of the self-sufficiency principle comparable to the invention of printing, namely photography and its allied arts. Even before the development of microphotography the Photostat had concentrated in this country many thousands of pages of records relating to the discovery, exploration, and colonization of America of which the originals are scattered among the archives and libraries of Europe, and had been used for the dissemination of other source materials such as eighteenth-century newspapers. Microphotography accelerated this process by greatly reducing the per-page cost. Any library may now have, at comparatively small expense, copies of English books to 1640, or of American books to 1800, or of the session papers of the British Parliament for the entire nineteenth century, of which no library, no matter how rich or ancient, has a complete set of originals, which are not available at any price. Photography has contributed to local self-sufficiency in other ways also, especially through facilitating the reprinting of out-of-print works, whether by photolithography or by mechanisms such as the Xerox Copy-Flo.

Printing and photography have thus, each in its turn, made it easier for research libraries to attain a measure of local self-sufficiency. Indeed, if the library's interest be sufficiently specialized, complete local self-sufficiency, in terms of comprehensiveness, may actually be attainable. But for the general research library this is not true.

No such library, no matter how vast its resources, can possess more than a fraction of what is produced.

We do not even know with any degree of accuracy how much is produced. For reasons into which it is unnecessary to go here, the statistics of world book production are very imperfect. A beginning at a systematic census was made at the Library of Congress some years ago but was not kept up. This estimated annual world production at the time to be in excess of 300,000 books, 70,000 periodicals, 30,000 newspapers, 17,000 maps, etc.[7] Meanwhile, from the fragmentary evidence supplied by the literatures of particular subjects (such as chemistry) or forms of publication (such as trade books or government documents), there is little doubt that total production continues to increase at a rapid rate, as it has since the first invention of printing, or even of writing.

Now, though the impracticability of comprehensiveness may thus be acknowledged, yet it would appear that local self-sufficiency should bear some quantitative as well as qualitative relationship to comprehensiveness, though the proportion might differ from place to place and from time to time. To serve its users adequately, a local collection must represent some significant fraction of the total available, and experience indicates that, to the extent of its users' interests, the larger this fraction is, the better. Thus, in an effort to maintain or increase

. . . .

[7] U.S. Library of Congress, *Information Bulletin* 13:43:App. (October 25, 1954); 14:5:11 (January 31, 1955); 14:16:App. (April 18, 1955). See also *Publisher's Weekly*, January 22, 1945, p. 352.

the numerical simultaneously with the qualitative fraction represented by their collections, the ten largest American libraries increased their acquisition rate by 71 per cent between 1940 and 1960 — from 196,000 to 371,000 pieces a year. And one great general research library even within recent years and without apology asserted its ideal if unrealizable goal, "In short, it should have everything."[8]

But, of course, every library typically results from a pooling or sharing of resources on the part of the individuals who constitute its clientele. So now, by an extension of the same principle of sharing, access to resources can be still further multiplied by interinstitutional arrangements. This principle, again, has been reinforced from time to time by technological development as well as by conscious human organization and effort. It is necessary to mention only the more important of these developments in order to suggest the diversity of means through which the limits of the local library are extended.

The publication of catalogs and bibliographies undoubtedly comes at the head of this list, for these provide

. . . .

[8] "The ideal objective of such a library [as the subject of the article] is a complete record of human thought, emotion and action. Its collections should be developed without distinction as to language, date, place, and form of publication. In short, it should have everything. The limitations imposed upon us by a practical world should not make us lose sight of this ideal. Our collections should be made as comprehensive as our resources permit, and we should limit them in ways which will do the least injury to their permanent value." R. A. Sawyer, "Book Selection in the Reference Department of the New York Public Library," *College & Research Libraries* 6:20-22 (December, 1944), p. 20.

information regarding what is available, and — frequently — where. The union catalog, the union list, and the bibliographic center are but specialized forms of these. In our own day the applications of photolithography have greatly facilitated the reproduction of catalogs of special collections, thus making available to the users of many libraries the results of the collecting, cataloging, and indexing which were previously restricted to the users of the institution where the collection was made. And we are now witnessing the computer being applied to the further improvement of bibliographic publication — improvement in particulars of speed, cheapness, and of comprehensiveness which nevertheless possesses the capacity for selectivity.

The convenience, cheapness, and rapidity of travel, transportation, and communication have similarly greatly contributed to sharing of resources. Quite aside from the recently won ability to spend a few weeks each summer in a distant library instead of waiting for a sabbatical year, the humble delivery truck which circulates among the libraries of a research area immediately extends the resources of each at the cost of but a few hours in service time.

Interlibrary lending and photocopying services remain, of course, the archetypes and symbols of sharing, those which are most familiar to the users of libraries, who for the most part have no conception of the elaborate arrangements in bibliographic standardization and organization and in interinstitutional comity upon which these so seemingly obvious services rest.

And finally, in a logical if not altogether in a chronological sense, must be mentioned the deliberate attempts to share responsibilities in acquisition by which libraries subordinate their own requirements for local self-sufficiency in the interest of the sufficiency of the larger community.

The effectiveness of all these arrangements has, in one sense, been extraordinary. Given sufficient time, patience, and some few funds to meet interlibrary loan, photocopying, and occasional searching fees, together with the assistance of an intelligent local librarian, it is quite possible to prosecute even complicated research with a considerable degree of success from almost any point in the United States and in many other places, commanding for the purpose the resources not only of the libraries of the country involved but also of much of the library-developed world besides.

But this is the bright side of the coin. Its other side is not so shiny. The fact is that dependence upon the resources of a distant library involves so much in the way of formalities, delay, cost, and the frustration and indignity of having one's request subordinated protractedly or absolutely to the prior claims of the immediate users of that library, as to make local self-sufficiency infinitely preferable, even though this may mean the stockpiling of large quantities of materials of prospectively little use, the construction of buildings of increasing inefficiency in which to store them, the costs of cataloging them, and the further costs of developing special storage arrangements for the less-used portions when the storage facilities become congested.

The picture that I have painted up to this point is

not a cheerful one. It is one in which the production of recorded communication vastly exceeds in quantity the capacity of individual libraries to acquire and control and in which the measures which are taken to share the wealth, heroic though they be, interpose enormous obstacles to this sharing.

But surely, we may say, just as inventiveness and organization have in the past continuously improved the conditions for local self-sufficiency and for sharing the resources, so they may be expected to serve the future. Before attempting to justify this faith, let us ask the prior question, What is it that we expect of the research library?

The Role of the Research Library

Stated in the simplest terms, the function of the research library is to enable inquirers to identify library materials relevant to their inquiries and to supply them with copies of these materials for their use.

Because in the general research library these inquiries reflect wide variations in subject, in depth of interest, in manner of approach, and in familiarity with library materials and methods, the library provides, in the first place, an elaborate and costly bibliographic apparatus to assist in identifying relevant materials, and it complements this apparatus with a reference service to assist inquirers in the exploitation of the apparatus and to compensate for some of its deficiencies.

Now the interesting thing about this bibliographic apparatus is that by far the most expensive part of it —

the library's own catalog — provides access only to that uniquely composed fraction of the world's literature which is represented by that particular library's collection. Indeed, the catalog doesn't even perform this function thoroughly: the library and its users are dependent upon the published bibliographies and indexes for the analysis of many of the volumes in its collection. In any one year, for example, there will typically be many more entries in these published indexes that are applicable to the library's collections than there will be new entries in its own catalog. (This situation is of course particularly conspicuous in libraries — of medicine or law for instance — where a large proportion of the stock is composed of serials, typically analyzed through published bibliographies and indexes rather than by the locally constructed catalog.)

And while this expensive search tool of the library's own making thus only imperfectly identifies the contents of only the locally available fraction of the world's literature, the library and its users must rely for knowledge of all the world's literature besides upon published sources—bibliographies, bibliographies of bibliographies, catalogs and indexes, and the too often fortuitous citations and references found in the locally available books; or upon sources outside the library itself.

For some areas of study, it is true, these tools are very effective (in spite of the complaints of their users) and provide the basis for the work of entire professions or industries, such as law or chemistry. But, in general, their use, as well as their actual availability to an inquirer, is obstructed by their very number, by their very considerable cost, by their laggardness in appearance, and by the duplications and omissions as between publications serving the same interest. A principal failing which they possess is the lack of a perspicuous system in over-all organization, leaving the inquirer uncertain as to what are the important bibliographies in the field or where they may be shelved. Add to this that the identification, through the published bibliographies, of relevant material not locally available merely marks the beginning of an all too laborious effort to gain access to it by purchase, loan, or photocopy, and it becomes fairly obvious that the published bibliographic apparatus, which in theory serves as the window through which the local library looks out upon that part of the world's literature which it does not possess, is in fact a very obscure porthole.

The proof of the pudding is in the eating. Research libraries pride themselves on their bibliographic collections, expend large sums in their maintenance, and devote large portions of their preferred space to displaying them, only to see them rarely used, unless and to the extent that they also analyze (as do the indexing and abstracting services) the local collection. Indeed, the use of these collections is not infrequently actually discouraged; the librarian, like the bookseller, is anxious to exploit the stock at hand rather than to invite requests for materials which must be procured from a distance. And what is true of the librarian is also true of the library's users; they will in general make shift with what is locally available rather than incur the inconvenience, cost, and uncertainty of doing better by relying upon distant sources.

The acceptance of the high cost of the catalog of the library's own making thus becomes understandable. Whatever its defects or limitations, this catalog is at least usually both conspicuous in physical form and reasonably perspicuous in intent. This is to identify, under principal rubrics, even though with certain important yet comprehensible reservations, the relevant portions of the world's literature that are locally available. For the immediate accessibility which is thus provided, a high cost is justified.

This would argue that the ability of the research library to fulfill its functions of identification and provision of relevant material is to a large degree controlled by the extent to which it has these materials at hand, displayed in its own catalog. In these terms the "In short, it should have everything" ambition becomes both understandable and reasonable.

But perhaps this is tommyrot. We all know that effective library service can be rendered with very restricted collections, that no man in his lifetime can read more than a tiny fraction of the literature even of his specialty. Why then this concern for more than a careful selection, made with regard to local needs and capacity to pay?

The answer lies not only in the nature of scholarly research, but increasingly in the nature of all human activity, especially at the point at which mankind has now arrived: in his industrial and commercial activities; in the arrangements with which he governs his relations to his fellows, locally, nationally, and internationally; in his relationships with the universe of nature upon which he is dependent.

Exactitude is one of the hallmarks of scholarship. But exactitude is impossible without access to sources. How often the secondary text proves corrupt! How often the footnote citation, traced to its source, fails to support the statement that it seemed to imply! How still more often are the meaningful details abridged! For the truth one must go to the sources.

But exactitude is no monopoly of scholarship. It is, in increasing measure, a requirement of all human activity. Gone are the days when a vessel could point vaguely into the west and expect to arrive in a homeland and a haven. No longer will a mere gift of eloquence together with a smattering of Blackstone assure success at the bar. No longer can the physician hope to bury his mistakes without fear of a suit for malpractice. Indulgent nature has allowed man, slaphappy and selfish, to squander her gifts through the centuries as though they were inexhaustible. She begins to withdraw, to insist that he measure his actions at his peril, to know what he is doing, and to make fuller use of his experience.

With the achievements of exact measurement in the physical sciences and technologies, and with their increasingly stringent requirements for exactitude, the beginning student soon becomes familiar. The national standard for time is held to an accuracy of fifteen-millionths of one part out of one million. A device is on the market which will measure the added weight of an encyclopedia after two words have been written on the margin of one of its pages. A search for similar exactness proceeds in the social sciences. Unfortunately, much of this exactitude is so technical in nature and at such a level of mathematical sophistication as too often to serve as an excuse for ignorance of it by those, including voters and legislators, whose decisions should benefit from exact knowledge. Meanwhile, in our anxiety to provide growing minds with the widest possible range of information in interesting and palatable forms, we are likely to oversimplify, to hand out pat and undocumented answers, and to stifle the critical faculty. I confess to being a little suspicious of school libraries, just because they are so good! In them one can find all the answers so easily and so unprovocatively! A little hard digging for facts in the literature of disagreement can be greatly conducive to the development of a skepticism which is not only healthy, but which has always been, and now if ever is, essential.

Accordingly, the trend, of which there is increasing evidence, of putting students on their own, of sending them to the literature, cannot be too highly commended.[9] But if this intellectual challenge is to succeed, the response must not be allowed, for want of adequate resources, to terminate at dogmatic assertions or ipse dixits, or to be estopped by untraceable genealogies of citations. This argues that the sources must be available.

I find it inescapable, in consequence, that if the general research library is in the future to fulfill its function, it must be able to provide its users with immediate access to local collections which will represent an increasingly significant fraction of the total available, and that it will

....
[9] I am informed by its librarian that the students in the Rutgers University Law School, who averaged two hours a week in the library twenty years ago, now average eighteen.

depend less and less upon sharing of resources *unless* means can be devised to make access through sharing comparable in effectiveness with access based on local availability.

If this conclusion is correct, then — unless we are prepared to support the local self-sufficiency principle by present methods through enormous expenditures for books, cataloging, and storage space — two lines of development are indicated: toward techniques for increased self-sufficiency at costs lower than those at present; or toward methods of sharing resources comparable with local availability. Let us briefly explore the apparent possibilities in each of these.

II

· ·

Extension
of Local
Self-Sufficiency

As described above, the principal developments which have hitherto contributed toward the local self-sufficiency of libraries have been the reproductive techniques — the arts of the copyist, of printing, and more recently of photography. Can further developments be expected along this line?

It has occurred to many that if photographic miniaturization could be pressed several orders beyond the point at which it is now employed, benefits might accrue to libraries. In the second lecture in this series a development of this kind was mentioned by Dr. Ralph R. Shaw — an experiment in 300-diameter microreproduction instead of the normal 10 to 20.[1]

Now the nature of the advantage that would accrue from such high-ratio miniaturization should be clearly understood: it would only adventitiously be an advantage in space-saving. The additional space that would be

· · · · · · · ·

[1] Ridenour, *op. cit.*, pp. 45-46.

saved over present reduction ratios would be unimportant and would probably in any case be devoured by the devices used to consult the microreproductions. For example, at a 10-diameter reduction the reduced image occupies only 1 per cent of the area occupied by the original and the (area) space-saving is 99 per cent. At a 100-diameter reduction the area of the images is reduced to one-tenth of 1 per cent of the original and the saving is 99.9 per cent. But to gain the additional nine-tenths of 1 per cent has required the transition from a comparatively easy technique to a very difficult one. Space-saving, then, is not the reason for using high-ratio reduction.

The real advantages should derive not from space-saving, but from inexpensiveness of dissemination. Let us suppose, for example, that an 8″ x 10″ photographic print costs $1. At a 10-diameter reduction, this print could hold the images of 100 8″ x 10″ original pages, and the per-page cost would be 1¢. At a 100-diameter reduction, the print would hold 10,000 images, and even if the cost of the print were doubled (because of the extra care required in processing), the per-page cost would still be only .02¢. At a 200-diameter reduction the print would hold 40,000 images, and if the cost of the print were now tripled over its original price, the per-page cost would still be only .0075¢. Such prices, if indeed obtainable, should reinforce the self-sufficiency principle comparably to printing or to microtext, at present, both of which typically provide book materials in the range of .2¢ to 3¢ a page. At the 200-diameter price suggested above, and neglecting the original cost of microfilming as well as the cost of the equipment for storing and giving service on the material, the prints for a library of a million 250-page books would cost $18,750.

A number of obstacles stand in the way. A first group of these relates to the making of microreductions at high ratios. Even at presently normal ratios, and even at the price of 1¢ a page, the cost of microfilming a million 250-page books would be $2.5 million, which would, presumably, be shared by the purchasers of prints. But the techniques for producing microreductions at high ratios are still at the stage of laboratory development. Enormously high resolution (thousands of lines per millimeter) is required of the optical system and of the photosensitive material, in addition to an allowance for loss in subsequent generations of copies, if the information contained in the original is to be adequately transcribed into print. And at these reduction ratios, dust and vibration interpose major impediments.

A next group of obstacles relates to the use of such microimages after they have been made. They obviously may not be touched by human hands. The cost of the elaborate equipment needed for projecting them for use might, however, well nullify the savings obtained by the reduction. Under these circumstances it might seem best to keep the collection of microimages intact, and to produce copies for use only on demand. This is what is accomplished by the Verac device, constructed by the AVCO Corporation. Here the images representing a 140-diameter reduction never leave the machine; a designated image can be located in a fraction of a second and can then either be projected on a television screen,

or reproduced on microfilm, or printed out on paper in
original size.[2] But again, the cost of the system tends to
nullify the savings for which it was constructed. If the
resultant paper print, including its share of the cost of
the equipment, were to cost only 5¢ a page, it might
have been better to have purchased an original — at
least of that particular book. A question for which no
answer can at this point be provided is, Would the local
availability of (let us say) a million seldom-used volumes
in microform justify the cost of 5¢ a page for those
which might be used? Would it justify the cost of 10¢
a page?

I am inclined to think that this problem will be solved
in the following manner. Though no one will willingly
pay 5¢ a page for a book which he might not use after
seeing it, he might be willing to pay 1¢ a page, especially
if by so doing he could avoid the delay and cost of securing a loan or photocopy elsewhere. Now it might be
possible to make enlargements from high-reduction
microtext for 1¢ a page, not at the full scale of the
original, but at, say, a 20-diameter reduction from the
original — in other words, in a format which would be
that of microtext at present reduction ratios. Such an
enlargement could then be used in the library's normal
microform viewers. For use outside the library, portable
reading devices are coming on the market which may
eventually overcome present obstacles to private individual use of microtext at the 20-diameter reduction.

In summary, it is my opinion that a principal present

. . . .
[2] Council on Library Resources, *Annual Report* 6:25-28
(1962).

obstacle to the profitable use of high-reduction microtext is the lack of an adequate reading device for individual use at the 20-diameter level; and that the solution of this problem will provide an enormous release to the use of microtext both at currently normal and at high reductions.

Before leaving the consideration of obstacles to this method of enriching collections, it might be well to mention copyright. Of course, dissemination of library material in microcopy at high reductions might be limited to material (of which there is no dearth) in which the copyright had expired or which was never copyrighted. This would, however, be limiting. It is nevertheless possible that reasonable arrangements might be made with copyright proprietors of materials which, though still protected, were inactive. It might even be found possible, by providing a publisher with a large market through dissemination in high-reduction photocopy, to reward him adequately and still to reduce the per-page cost of his publication to the recipients. But these are all matters for future investigation.

Dr. Shaw, in mentioning the then recent experiments in 300-diameter reduction, immediately dismissed it. Is the basic problem, he inquired, one of putting a million-volume library at a scholar's fingertips? The critical factor would appear to be, he concluded, not primarily one of physical proximity to a maximum number of volumes, but a means for determining what volumes exist, and for obtaining those volumes for the scholar as required.[3]

. . . .

[3] Ridenour, *loc. cit.*

This comment, I think, failed to discriminate between the value of miniaturizing for the mere sake of space-saving, and its value in facilitating dissemination and in the consequent local availability of books. As stated above, the first is not worth the candle; but the importance of the second would appear, from the experience of libraries throughout history, to be paramount.

However, with the conclusion that the critical factor is a means of determining what volumes exist, there can be no quarrel. This is basic. Let us turn to it for a moment.

THE MICROLIBRARY AND THE CATALOG; BROWSING, WEEDING, PRESERVATION

Little purpose is served by the acquisition of material which lies uncataloged or which is cataloged by inferior methods. It follows that, if a general research library should greatly extend its holdings, even of less-used material, through massive acquisitions of high-reduction microtext, its readers should be given the same opportunities for identifying relevant material among them as if they were originals.

Actually, this might not prove difficult. By definition, high-ratio photoreproduction is a technique of dissemination, of publication. Presumptively, were a million-volume library available in this form, a number of libraries might subscribe. This, then, would provide the conditions justifying the publication of a catalog in book form which would give no less full cataloging treatment to the microtexts than if they were originals, and of

which the cost to each subscriber would be but a fraction
of that which would result from an attempt to catalog
the collection by itself. Presumptively, also, such a catalog would conspicuously complement the library's own
catalog, and would at least equal it in perspicuity of
function and organization. Furthermore, it could be
consulted with even more assurance, for everything listed
therein would always be available; nothing in the micro-
store could be misplaced, on loan, or in the bindery.

Admittedly, there are several important "ifs" in this
scheme. But if there were no "ifs" the future would be
with us now, and there would be no point in the present
exercise. And the "ifs" which interpose to the realization of the scheme do not seem to me to be ineluctable.

Granting, then, the possible realization of the "ifs,"
let us look just a little further into the future. High-
reduction microphotography will have made it possible,
let us say, for the general research library to make
enormous additional strides, at reasonable cost, toward
local self-sufficiency. The same technique should also
assist it in controlling the size and disposition of its collections.

A recent study has concluded that the present economics of microfilming leave it on the whole better to
retain an original volume than to attempt, by substituting
a microcopy for it, to reduce storage costs, even if a
number of other libraries should participate in the effort.[4]
The study concludes with the proviso, however, that this

. . . .
[4] V. W. Clapp and R. T. Jordan, "Re-evaluation of Microfilm as a Method of Book Storage," *College & Research Libraries*
24:5-15 (January, 1963).

situation might be radically altered if high-ratio micro-reproduction processes should become practical.

If, as we are assuming here, microtext editions should be able to compete by a significant margin of cost with the storage of originals and still permit convenient use, the storage library would no longer hold much meaning. Every decade or so, the subscribing libraries could agree upon the lesser-used books to be retired to microtext; an edition would be published together with a catalog in book form (perhaps updating the catalogs of previous decades), and the shelves and catalogs of the subscribing libraries could be weeded. Thus the collection of originals of these libraries could be kept within the bounds of whatever millions of original volumes the future shows to be optimum for a research library. Neither bibliographical access nor physical access would be lost, and the task of altering the catalog records to show the new locations of books removed to storage would be obviated.

One important facility currently afforded by many general research libraries would probably be lost — that of browsing. I believe this to be important. I am not impressed by the arguments that state that much material is already out of reach of browsing — that it is buried in articles in journals or is already in microform, or does not exist in the library in which the browsing takes place. My experience satisfies me that browsing in a collection in which the books are arranged in systematic order is a valuable method of access.[5]

. . . .
[5] "The advantages of close classification for . . . a large collection of books will be apparent to any librarian. . . . And time and again it has been found, in seeking information, or compil-

Consequently, I believe that every effort should be made to compensate for the reduced facility of browsing consequent upon withdrawing books for storage whether in a storage library or in microform. One possibly feasible way of doing this is to provide a classed catalog of the withdrawn titles. There may be other ways.[6]

Let me introduce still another consideration. In one of his last attendances at a national library meeting, Dr. William Warner Bishop, then one of the grand old men of American librarianship, appeared before the Association of Research Libraries in Buffalo in June, 1946, to urge that action be taken to preserve the rapidly deteriorating books of the wood-pulp paper period.[7] Not until 1957 was a concerted attack made on this problem, commencing with a study to ascertain the present condition of books printed in the twentieth century. This study showed that the average American nonfiction book paper of the first decade of the century retains only 4 per cent

. . . .
ing subject lists on request, that scrutiny of books on the shelves produces a far more satisfactory answer than a compiling of lists from bibliographies and other works of reference. Thus, on the shelves, it is possible to bring to light the concealed bibliography, or the unexpectedly full historical introduction, which is not referred to in the secondhand source." C. G. Walters, "Cataloguing in the Department of Printed Books, National Library of Wales," *Library Association Record* 65:151-155 (April, 1963), p. 153.

[6] It was hoped that the Yale University Library study of its Selective Book Retirement Program might shed useful light on this problem, but the other aspects of the study have so far monopolized its attention. Council on Library Resources, *Annual Report* 3:33 (1959).

[7] Association of Research Libraries, *Minutes* 25:6 (June 19, 1946).

of the strength of a typical new book paper, while publications even of the 1940's had already lost 64 per cent of what is presumed to have been their original strength. In short, few of the books of the first half of this century may be expected to be usable by its end.[8]

In 1960 the Association of Research Libraries took the action urged by Dr. Bishop in 1946 and appointed a Committee on Preservation of Research Library Materials. As its first task this committee undertook to estimate the quantities of the materials that would be involved in a preservation program. A statistical study was made, based upon entries in the National Union Catalog. This gave an estimate of the number of separate books (not including serials) in American libraries represented in the Catalog printed before 1870, the effective beginning of the wood-pulp paper period, together with a breakdown by decade of publications and country of origin. The total number of pages was estimated at approximately 1.75 billion.[9]

The committee is now wrestling with the problem of what to do about these 1.75 billion pages, many — perhaps most — of which are doomed within a relatively brief foreseeable future. There are a number of alternatives. A method of chemical treatment, using a fine

. . . .

[8] W. J. Barrow and R. J. Sproull, "Permanence in Book Papers," *Science* 129:1075-84 (April 24, 1959); R. W. Church, ed., *Deterioration of Book Stock: Causes and Remedies. Two Studies on the Permanence of Book Paper Conducted by W. J. Barrow* (Richmond: Virginia State Library, 1959).

[9] E. E. Williams, "Magnitude of the Paper-Deterioration Problem as Measured by a National Union Catalog Sample," *College & Research Libraries* 23:499, 543 (November, 1962).

spray, is being perfected that promises to delay deterioration almost indefinitely; but this will be comparatively expensive (perhaps a dollar or more per volume).[10] Exploration is also proceeding of the possibility of preserving at least one archival copy through storage at reduced temperatures, it having been tentatively found that a drop of 20° C. in storage temperature will multiply the expected life of paper by a factor of approximately 7.5.[11] But in any plan for preservation the applicability of microreproduction necessarily receives high consideration: it is comparatively inexpensive; it reduces storage, binding, and other maintenance costs; it permits inexpensive replication. (Against this it must be said that it is not very durable and that its permanence still remains to be proven.) Furthermore, it is already the standard method for preserving newspapers, and many libraries have extensive microfilm preservation programs for books as well.

It would appear in consequence that, even if alternative methods should be used to some degree, the probability is that a major part of the preservation task will be performed by microphotography. What will happen then? Will the negatives be held, in a national repository or by the libraries which performed the microfilming, as a source of service copies? Will each deteriorated original be replaced by a film copy? (It may be pointed out that, unless the deteriorated copies are replaced, the initially holding libraries will lose more than just their

. . . .

[10] Council on Library Resources, *Annual Report* 6:22 (1962).
[11] L. E. Grove, "What Good Is Greenland?" *Wilson Library Bulletin* 16:749-750 (May, 1962).

originals: they will lose — and at further cost — the cataloging investment which they made in these originals, unless they are willing to permit entries to remain in their catalogs for books which are no longer immediately available.

The sensible solution to look to is, again, a solution based upon replacement of originals by high-reduction microfacsimile, accompanied by publication of full cataloging information. Such a solution would simultaneously accomplish, with preservation, an important extension of the bibliographic and physical access which is afforded by immediate availability.

In the absence of practical methods for making and employing high-reduction microfacsimile, the committee obviously cannot at the present time adopt this solution. However, it can prepare for it. It is probable that high-reduction microfacsimiles, if made, will be produced by further reduction of microfilm employing normal reduction ratios. To be suitable for this purpose, however, such microfilm must be of high quality, both with respect to resolution and other characteristics. This argues that not only microfilm preservation programs, but all library microfilming programs should contemplate the use of the product at further reductions.

The preservation of color-printing in originals presents still a further problem. Some attention has been paid to it, but there is little that can definitely be stated at the present time.[12]

Meanwhile, a still further prospect of improvement
. . . .
[12] Clapp and Jordan, *loc. cit.*

appears in this connection. Since the mid-1920's the completion of the National Union Catalog has been an objective of research library effort, and much energy has been expended toward its achievement. But it still falls short of the goal: the research holdings of the country are still far from being completely of record.

But if projects should take shape for massive dissemination in microfacsimile, accompanied by full cataloging in book form, it is foreseeable that this would provide an enormous stimulus to the discovery of books now in the country but not recorded. At the same time, the very dissemination of these massive microform collections and the accompanying catalogs would provide an automatic record of location.

III

. . . .

Extension
of the
Sharing Principle

Local self-sufficiency is, as we have seen, a goal justifying much effort and expense. Yet it may be admitted
that it is not likely ever to be completely attainable.
Even if inexpensive methods of dissemination, such as
those described above, should become feasible, there will
undoubtedly always be materials which are not yet generally disseminated. There will probably always be, in
addition, categories of specialized material (e.g., of an
archival character) which by general consent should not
be so disseminated.

Sharing the resources may, in consequence, be expected to persist among even the great general research
libraries. But, no less important, these libraries share
their resources with lesser libraries which do not and will
not possess the same approximations to self-sufficiency.
For all these reasons the effort to improve the techniques
of sharing of resources must not be neglected. Indeed,
if techniques for sharing could be developed which
would provide even in some areas an adequacy of service

comparable to that afforded by immediate availability, they would to that extent render the high costs of local self-sufficiency unnecessary.

Furthermore, it is noteworthy that conscious group planning for sharing of resources is a fairly recent development, most of which has fallen into the past century or even half century, and that there is even more general interest and incentive at the present time for the improvement of these arrangements than ever in the past. It is not inconceivable that the sharing principle might rapidly overtake the local self-sufficiency principle.

Thirteen years ago Dean Ridenour pointed out that the sums devoted annually to acquisition by the major libraries of this country would support what he called "a rather fancy" communication system, leaving over a sum larger than that available to any single library.[1] No one yet has taken up this challenge and attempted to work out the situations in which communication might be able to substitute effectively for local availability.

Let us see what can be done. What we seek is improvements of the arrangements, first, by which the existence of relevant materials not locally available becomes known to the inquirer, and, second, by which copies of these materials are brought to his desk.

BIBLIOGRAPHIC ACCESS

The first of these desiderata concerns the bibliographical arrangements. How may these be improved to promote sharing of resources?

. . . .

[1] Ridenour, *op. cit.*, pp. 21-22.

The obvious first step is through the improvement of union catalog services. It has been apparent for some time that union catalogs suffer from an inadequate technology that reduces their efficiency at all stages — the assembly, editing, recording, weeding, and servicing of the units of information of which they are composed. In 1962 the National Union Catalog received from 763 libraries 1,338,000 entries which then had to be reduced to a much smaller number by methods involving not merely interfiling, but also the recognition of variant entries for the same books. As a result of these processes half a million cards were filed into the supplements to the main Catalog and 170,000 cards into the main Catalog itself. In contrast to this massive editing and filing operation was the number of requests searched: these stood at under 33,000 titles.[2]

If resources are to be shared in fact as well as in name, the technology of maintaining union catalogs obviously requires improvement: they must be able to represent more completely the available resources; to represent the total cataloging of these holdings and not merely main entries; to reflect the weedings as well as the acquisitions of the participants; and to supply the information thus assembled conveniently and promptly to inquirers in any part of the country. Improvement in these respects has been effected in regard to recent publications by the book-form *National Union Catalog*, but this of course has not affected the record of older publications.

. . . .
[2] U.S. Library of Congress, *Annual Report* 1962:15, 16, 123.

A subcommittee of the Resources Committee of the
American Library Association is wrestling with these
problems. From its efforts may result further improvements. The most obvious method is through editing and
publication in book form of the National Union Catalog
for titles prior to 1956. However, there are alternatives.
One of these is publication in microform. This method
has been adopted for the Slavic Union Catalog; it will
be interesting to observe experience with its use. Another
is based upon the possible application of computer techniques.

There can be little doubt that methods will gradually
be found for employing computers or computer-like machines in the operations of libraries. The general out-
lines of the problems of such applications are gradually
becoming clear in such general studies as those at the
Chicago Undergraduate Division of the University of
Illinois[3] and at the Library of Congress[4] in addition to
numerous special studies. We may, in consequence, expect within the foreseeable future at least the initial
availability of cataloging information in machine-
readable form.

It is a characteristic of information in this form that
it can be reproduced, arranged, and rearranged at high
speeds and comparatively low cost. Now, several hun-
dred research libraries in the United States already have
access to the computer type of equipment with which
such operations are performed, but a principal reason
....
[3] L. A. Schulteiss and others, *Advanced Data Processing in
the University Library* (New York: Scarecrow Press, 1962).
[4] U.S. Library of Congress, *Annual Report* 1962:xiii.

for the neglect of these devices by these libraries is that there is as yet no convenient source of bibliographic information in the required machine-readable form. If the Library of Congress catalog were made available in such form (the feasibility of which is being explored in the study just referred to), prospects for the mechanization of bibliographic information would rapidly open up. Individual libraries could copy from the Library of Congress catalog and at the same time add a record of such of their own holdings as were not represented. A national union catalog in machine-readable form might quickly take shape — a national union catalog which, benefiting from the experience of the past, might become much more useful than anything now available. For such improved usefulness this catalog should reflect the full and not merely the main-entry cataloging of the participating libraries, thus making available to all the intellectual analysis which is now restricted to local clienteles. It should be possible not only to update and to weed this catalog electronically at long distance, but also to consult it electronically from any point in the country.

The spark needed to fire the succession of developments leading to this result is very simple — it is the commencement of the conversion of a great catalog to machine-readable form. Although conditions are not quite ripe for this, they are impending. Before speaking further of the possibilities here, let us turn to another aspect of the improvement of the arrangements for bibliographic access for sharing of resources.

The published bibliographical services upon which libraries depend for access to the contents of their serials, as well as to certain other materials such as government publications, also serve as a basis for sharing resources by identifying materials which are not locally available. The improvement of these services, in promptness, coverage, avoidance of duplication, presentation, and cost has been the subject of endless discussions. Although research libraries provide a considerable share of the support of these services, they do not typically participate in the publishing decisions which are capable of passing on to them the cost of bibliographic archaisms. Although the American Library Association's prewar attempt to stimulate coordination among these services ended in failure,[5] the time may be ripe for a renewed display of interest.

However, in the case of one of these services (significantly, produced by a library) an impressive effort has been and is being made to overcome the defects just mentioned by making use of the most advanced techniques. I refer to the *Index Medicus* and to the current project for employing a computer in its production. A great many lessons both for bibliographic publication as well as for the organization of research library services can be studied from this effort; at this moment I would comment upon just one aspect, namely its relation to the availability of cataloging information in machine-readable form.

Hitherto, the machine processing of bibliographic data has been severely constrained by the limited type fonts

. . . .

[5] Joint Committee on Indexing and Abstracting in the Major Fields of Research, "Final Report," *ALA Bulletin* 39:370-371, 426-427 (October 15, 1945).

(usually restricted, for example, to upper-case type) available to the data-processing mechanisms. So long as these limitations exist, it would be of little value to convert a large body of bibliographical data at large expense to machine-readable form.

The success of the *Index Medicus* project, however, is dependent upon its ability to command a type font of adequate size as well as a high degree of presentability and a high rate of speed in printing. In order to secure these capabilities, it has had to break new ground.[6] It may be expected that the accomplishment, which now seems to be assured, will hasten the advent of general bibliographical information in machine-readable form, and consequently the possibility of union catalogs which may be maintained and consulted electronically in the manner which I have suggested above.

At this point one may well ask, If electronically consultable files can replace the present card files of union catalogs, will they not similarly replace the published bibliographic services, especially those which, because of the quantity of the literature which they attempt to analyze, have become excessively large, complex, and costly? Will not the chemist, the lawyer, and the medical scientist secure their bibliographic references by wire from specialized information centers, and everyone else perhaps from the H. W. Wilson Company? There are certainly those who are thinking in these terms,[7] but we

. . . .

[6] General Electric Company, Defense Systems Department, Information Systems Operation, *The MEDLARS Story* (Bethesda, Md., 1962), pp. 2-34, 35, 36; 3-9, 10.

[7] E.g., John G. Kemeny, "A Library for 2000 A.D.," *in* Martin

must be content to leave these developments to the future. An intermediate step may be such as is planned by the *Index Medicus,* in which the published bibliographic service will provide an analysis of the literature to a certain level (e.g., not to exceed a predesignated number of subject entries per title) while a much more refined analysis will be retained to make possible a more thorough processing of bibliographic inquiries, by machine, than would be possible with the published bibliography.[8]

Before leaving the subject of bibliographic access it is, however, appropriate to mention the possibilities of cataloging and indexing by machine. In the second Windsor Lecture Dean Ridenour stated that it is probably the steps involved in analytical bibliography that would first engage the attention of an open-minded engineer determined to reduce library costs and raise library efficiency.[9] After the establishment of the Council on Library Resources, I wrote to Dean Ridenour, then at the Lockheed Aircraft Corporation, reminding him of this. He responded with a proposal for research, and he and I were due to discuss this on his visit to Washington in May, 1959, during which his death occurred.

However, an investigation of the possibilities was undertaken by another physicist, Dr. Don R. Swanson, then of Thompson Ramo Wooldridge, Inc., and now expiating this introduction to library problems as the director

. . . .

Greenberger, ed., *Management and the Computer of the Future* (Cambridge: MIT Press, 1962), pp. 134-178.

[8] General Electric Company, *op. cit.,* pp. 2-7, 8; 3-3.

[9] Ridenour, *op. cit.,* p. 27.

of a principal graduate library school. Suffice it to say that there are now experimental results which promise successful subject indexing of natural text by data-processing machines at reasonable cost, providing that the text to be analyzed is available in machine-readable form.[10] Until such availability occurs, these indexing programs must remain of academic interest; but one can be sure that such availability will occur, presumably commencing in specific subject fields. At that time, if the computer indexing programs justify their promise, research libraries will benefit through the provision of perhaps cheaper, perhaps better, perhaps prompter, or perhaps just more subject indexing.

Indeed, the data-processing mechanisms are already contributing to the bibliographic apparatus of libraries. The technique of the concordance, now mechanized, has made this kind of index a work of days instead of years. Under the name of "permuted" or "key-word-in-context" index, it has brought to indexing the advantages of machine processing — rapidity, accuracy, cheapness, and low degree of demand upon human judgment. Such indexes are being used extensively where quick

. . . .

[10] D. R. Swanson, "Searching Natural Text by Computer," *Science* 132:1099-1104 (October 21, 1960); D. R. Swanson, "Interrogating a Computer in Natural Language," *in* International Federation for Information Processing, *Information Processing 1962. Proceedings of IFIP Congress 62* (Amsterdam: North-Holland Publishing Co., 1963), pp. 288-293; *Machine Indexing: Progress and Problems. Papers Presented at the Third Institute in Information Storage and Retrieval, February 13-17, 1961* (Washington, D.C.: American University, Center for Technology and Administration, [1962]).

access to recent literature is important, as in chemistry, biology, state legislation, etc.

So much for subject cataloging or indexing by machine. As for descriptive cataloging by machine, less can be said. It will be a long time before the complicated rules by which a descriptive catalog entry is produced can be reduced to a formula which can be entrusted to a machine.[11] There are better ways of improving descriptive cataloging than this, but I am not sufficiently sure that they will be adopted to be willing to risk a prediction regarding them in connection with the future of the research library.

In summary, improved sharing of resources is dependent in the first place upon improved means for identifying and locating copies of relevant material. This requires improvement of the bibliographic apparatus. There is much work to be done here, but there are prospects of assistance from technological developments.

PHYSICAL ACCESS

Let us turn to the second stage of the sharing process, the stage at which copies of materials which have been identified as potentially relevant are brought to the desk of the inquirer.

Can we improve the methods by which this is normally accomplished, namely interlibrary loan or photocopy? There are some indications that we can.

....
[11] D. R. Swanson, "Library Goals and the Role of Automation," *Special Libraries* 53:466-471 (October, 1962).

There are several reasons for the unsatisfactory performance of interlibrary loan and photocopy services.
The first is the extent of the formalities. The amount of
paper work which must be performed before an interlibrary loan or photocopy order is completed is several
times greater than if the same material were available
locally. Efforts have been made to reduce these formalities, through adoption of codes of practice and stan-
dardized multipart forms. Under some circumstances
teletype is found effective. But the formalities remain
burdensome. If interlibrary loan or photocopy requests
could be placed by mere reference to a numbered item
(e.g., in a book catalog), signed by the station identification of the requesting library, the red tape might be
further reduced. Here is something for a committee to
work on.

But still another obstacle derives from the lack of
obligation of the requested to the requesting library. The
borrower at a distance necessarily takes second place,
especially since he does not look up his own call
numbers.

One method for improving this situation is that which
is increasingly adopted in a number of states, where
allocations of state funds are made toward the strength-
ening of the collections of particular libraries upon the
specific condition that these libraries assume obligations
of service to others. In this matter of obligation it would
appear that American libraries may actually be behind
their colleagues in a number of the countries of conti-
nental Europe. Neither can the United States match
such British agencies as the National Central Library

and the National Lending Library for Science and Technology, whose exclusive function it is to provide a back-stopping service to the country as a whole.

But there is still a third obstacle to efficiency in sharing; it results from the scattering of materials. This scattering means loss of motion in speculating or ascertaining where relevant materials may be found. Not all requests can be sent to the few largest libraries. An acarologist in Berkeley once told me that he had to deal regularly with about seventy-one libraries in this country alone.

There is, however, at least one example of a library which is not only preeminent in its holdings, approaching comprehensiveness in a particular subject, but which also publishes a principal current bibliography of that subject and which has certain obligations for nation-wide service. This is the National Library of Medicine. It is but rarely necessary to inquire where material in the field covered by this library is located; the answer is automatic. Furthermore, the current bibliography which this library publishes is also its catalog; difficulties of identification are eliminated, and loans might be negotiated by a numerical designation as effectively as by full citation. Still further, this library is not oppressed by the needs of a local clientele. Lastly, it has developed efficient techniques for sharing the use of its collections when local resources have been exhausted. In 1961 it made more than 106,000 loans; of these (if the proportions of previous years' experience held true) 93 per cent were for serial material and 7 per cent nonserial; 15 per cent of the loans were outside and 85 per cent within the United States.[12]

Does this model offer suggestions for the improvement of arrangements for sharing resources? Suppose that assignments for comprehensive acquisition in major subjects could be made to specific institutions, each of which would also have responsibility for the current bibliography and also for a backstopping lending service in the subject; much clarity and order would then be introduced into a situation which is now characterized by confusion and disorder. Such tools as the National Union Catalog and the *Union List of Serials* would be rendered to a degree unnecessary, for one would automatically know where to turn for the literature of these subjects: for medicine here, agriculture there, chemistry there, law in still another place, etc.

While the National Library of Medicine offers the most conspicuous example of a national backstop to local library resources in a specific subject, there are many other less well-developed examples. Indeed, these are so numerous that the National Science Foundation has published a directory of them.[13] Their competence runs all the way from "abortion" to "zoology"; but — regretfully for my friend in Berkeley — they do not yet com-

. . . .

[12] W. H. Kurth, *Survey of the Interlibrary Loan Operation of the National Library of Medicine* ([Washington, D.C.]: U.S. Department of Health, Education, and Welfare, 1962).

[13] *Specialized Science Information Services in the United States: A Directory of Selected Specialized Information Services in the Physical and Biological Sciences.* ([Washington, D.C.]: National Science Foundation, [1961]).

prehend "acarology"; he must still presumably correspond with seventy-one libraries!

The fact is, however, that useful as these specialized information services may be to individual or institutional workers in the subject fields involved, they nevertheless represent for the most part merely additional bibliographic services which must be consulted by mail or telephone rather than in the form of published volumes on the local shelves. They will not genuinely become a part of the research library system and extend the resources of individual libraries comparably to the local possession of the materials involved until they embody the three elements which to a large degree characterize the service of the National Library of Medicine. These three elements, I repeat, are comprehensive acquisition within a conspicuous subject field; publication of the principal current bibliography of that field; and the obligation to backstop local resources in that field. To the extent that this pattern could be perfected and repeated, sharing of resources would become routinized, and the need for local self-sufficiency would be correspondingly reduced. Subjects to which this pattern might be extended will readily occur. Will librarians take the initiative toward such extension along the lines of the excellent model now existing, or will the development be left to others who may not so well comprehend the factors which are essential to an efficient system?

Assistance from Technological Developments

So far we have been talking about the administrative arrangements which promote effective physical access to needed materials through sharing of resources. To complete the picture we should also mention the assistance which may be expected from technological development. The delivery truck (in metropolitan areas) and air mail (between cities) have so expedited the transmission of material that little further remains to be accomplished. Much (perhaps most) of the time now required for securing material from a distance is attributable to the formalities, and perhaps the least part of it to actual time in shipment. Yet this time could be further reduced by development of electronic methods of transmission.

Telefacsimile has long offered an attractive possibility; for more than three decades it has been successfully used in newspaper work; why not also for libraries?

As typically used for wirephoto transmission, telefacsimile is unsuitable for libraries. There, material can be sent in single sheets which can be wrapped around a cylinder for transmission and similarly be recorded on another cylinder at the receiving terminal. Library material typically does not lend itself to such treatment but must be scanned flat. Furthermore, library material is typically acquired in multiples of pages rather than single sheets; and transmission at the low speeds which are satisfactory for wirephoto (and which permit the use of low-cost channels of narrow bandwidth) again becomes unsuitable.

Of course there are enormous commercial, industrial, and other pressures for improvement of telefacsimile in all these particulars. As far back as 1953 a flatbed scanner developed by the Radio Corporation of America for the Atomic Energy Commission was employed in a demonstration of telefacsimile between the Library of Congress and the National Institutes of Health.[14] This experiment found that the actual cost of the service (over a distance of some ten miles) was approximately the same as by delivery truck; but the lending library retained its originals and the receiving library obtained a disposable copy. However (aside from the imperfections of the machine) it was a *reductio ad absurdum* to employ an assistant to stand by all day watching the machine lazily scanning articles in journals while the whole pile of books could have been delivered by truck in an hour. Transmission time in that case was not reduced.

There has been considerable advance in equipment since then, and much has been learned as to the conditions under which the use of telefacsimile can be justified in terms of use and cost. A recent installation between the Franklin Institute in Philadelphia and an industrial library in Valley Forge, which is reported to have reduced the interlibrary loan lag from ten days to five minutes, may be instructive in some of these matters.[15]

It may be foreseen that the installation of telefacsimile between libraries would, by pointing up the distribution of time in the execution of loans, of itself exert great pressure to reduction of the time spent in the formalities. On the other hand, however, to the extent that the transmitting and receiving terminals require special supervision, this cost (added to the cost of the equipment,

. . . .

[14] S. Adams, "Facsimile for Federal Libraries," *Special Libraries* 44:169-172 (May-June, 1953).

[15] "Pennsylvania Libraries Experiment with Electronic Facsimile System," *Library Journal* 88:1848-49 (May 1, 1963).

the rental of the channel, and the expense of the received "hard copy") will considerably disadvantage this technique in economic terms in comparison with loan of originals or provision of photocopies.

At a still further level of technological development, it is already possible to transmit informational records rapidly and inexpensively (in the order of 1,000 words per minute over ordinary telephone voice circuits, with much greater speeds over channels of wider bandwidth) provided that the information be in machine-readable form (e.g., on punched or magnetic tape). However, in spite of the inclusion of this technique in the ALA report on information networks of the future,[16] it may be doubted that it will profoundly affect the operations of research libraries at any early date, for lack of the basic machine-readable material.

. . . .

[16] American Library Association, *op. cit.*, p. 20.

IV

· ·

Data Processing—
Information Storage
and Retrieval

No supervisor of a general research library can afford, in these days, to ignore the approaches to the administration of information services which bear the labels affixed to the head of this chapter — "data processing" and "information storage and retrieval."

The labels are of postwar origin, though the concepts to which they refer are old. The discussions, research, and demonstrations to which these approaches have given rise have rediscovered many of the old truths of library work, but have also brought to bear the intelligence and enthusiasm of many scientists, engineers, and others whose interest would not have been excited by traditional methods of giving library service. At the same time, however, the practicing librarian is to a considerable degree baffled by these developments; he would like to make use of them, but is unsure how to proceed.

The two approaches are closely related. Information storage and retrieval has always been dependent upon devices, the earliest form of which was possibly the blaze cut on a tree along the forest path or stones piled atop each other in the open. So now this approach consciously seeks devices for more meaningful, more capacious, quicker, and cheaper recording and supply of information.

Data processing has similarly always been dependent upon devices; perhaps the fingers used in counting provide the primordial example. The two approaches come together when data which has been processed by mechanical devices is stored and supplied upon demand by devices which may be the same or different.

Not only have devices of both kinds been used in libraries since the beginning of time, but the materials of which libraries are formed are actually themselves information storage and retrieval devices representing the results of data processing. There is consequently in this situation nothing fundamentally new. What is new and baffling is the flood of new ideas and equipment which require for their evaluation an almost continuous review and restudy of the library's objectives and procedures. This is in no small part due to the fact that many of these devices combine at one and the same time fantastic capabilities of one kind with complete incapabilities in other respects. To reject an emperor's offer of an elephant might be rude, but it would probably require a complete revision of one's way of life to employ the elephant profitably.

To put the matter in perspective, it is important to emphasize continually the essential function of the research library. This is, as previously stated, to provide access in bibliographic and in physical terms to the records of human communication. Any device or system which contributes to the execution of that function is to be welcomed; otherwise, no matter how interesting it may be from the point of view of its promotion of intellectual activity generally, its effect upon library organization and operation is likely to be indirect rather than direct. Thus, the invention of the type-composing machines had an enormous indirect effect upon library service in the sense (for example) that they made the indexing services of the H. W. Wilson Company economically feasible; but these machines did not directly affect library operation in the sense of being introduced into libraries. So it will probably be with many of the developments now under way under the rubrics of "data processing" and "information storage and retrieval."

Specifically, many of the techniques now being elaborated for organizing, storing, and recovering information will find applicability in specialized information centers concerned with the refined analysis of the literature of a special field or with current research in that field. It is likely, too, that one of the current preoccupations of documentalists, namely classification theory, will similarly affect the organization of information in restricted rather than in wide fields. (This is not to say that the methods of cataloging and subject analysis now used by libraries may not be considerably improved, although the results of recent experiments would indicate that this will not be effected very easily.[1])

. . . .

[1] See, e.g., the reports of the ASLIB Cranfield Research Project in the Comparative Efficiency of Indexing Systems by Cyril W. Cleverdon: *Report on the First Stage* (Cranfield:

However, there can be little doubt that profound effects in the organization and operation of research libraries may be expected from current developments in data processing by automatic electronic devices. Some of these have been suggested above. A principal draw-back to the use of automatic data-processing mechanisms for research library applications in the past has resided in the comparative slow speed (in the face of the enor-mous quantities of bibliographic data contained in the files of research libraries) but more particularly in the poverty of type faces commanded by their printed prod-uct. As stated previously, both these objections are now on the way to elimination, and it may confidently be expected that the very near future will witness the com-mencement at long last (this has been a hope since the mid-1930's) of the availability from central sources of bibliographic information in adequate machine-readable form.

The situation may then be quite comparable to that which greeted the introduction of the Library of Con-gress printed catalog card in 1901. That so seemingly simple device was really a very sophisticated product, culminating many years of development. It reflected an international agreement in catalog card size; it repre-sented a national (and shortly thereafter an interna-tional) standard of cataloging rules; it conveyed to its purchasers at the mere price of stationery the results of the most elaborate cataloging and classification system
. . . .
College of Aeronautics, 1960); *Interim Report on the Test Pro-gramme* (1960); *Report on the Testing and Analysis of an Investigation* (1962).

up to that time devised. Much — perhaps most — of the country's cataloging and other bibliographic work is still being performed by means of this device, although comparatively little has been done to improve it over its condition at its initial appearance.

The central supply of bibliographic information in machine-readable form may be expected to have similarly important consequences. It may be expected that gradually the equipment for exploiting its capabilities will become very widely diffused. A principal capability will probably be found to be that of preparing printer's copy for book-format catalogs. What effect this may have on the local card catalog would be hard to say, but this effect might well be to abolish it, or at the very least make its contents available in multiple copies throughout the neighborhood and to reduce it to an interim record. The possible effect on union catalogs I have already suggested.

But this is only one of the possibilities which might result from the availability of bibliographic information in machine-readable form. Because all the substantive operations of libraries have to do with the basic bibliographic record, it may be expected that they will all be eventually affected, and there are already many experiments in this direction. It is foreseeable, also, that, endowed with this new capacity for easily producing and disseminating bibliographic information, research libraries may in the future much more than at present undertake to provide their users currently with information regarding the existence of materials relevant to their interests.

V

. . . .

Summary
and
Conclusion

I have proceeded, in the foregoing, from the premise
that the general research library of the future will increasingly be required to make available to its users the
informational records of mankind. To do this effectively,
it must not only be able to inform these users as to what
materials exist, but it must also be able to provide them
promptly with copies of those that they need. The single
best method of doing these things which has so far been
discovered is that of having a large collection at hand,
adequately cataloged. But since the still-increasing rate
of production of informational records will make it even
more difficult than now for libraries to acquire and
catalog significant portions of the total, other means
must be devised.

One way is by extension of the techniques which in
the past have made the major contribution to local self-
sufficiency, namely the techniques of inexpensive reproduction and dissemination. There seem to be genuine
possibilities that these can contribute not only to massive

increases in the collections of libraries at much lower costs than at present, but also to the effective cataloging of these collections, the disposition of lesser-used materials in the interest of efficient use of storage space, the preservation of deteriorating materials, and the improvement of union catalogs.

Another way is through improvement of the arrangements, developed for the most part during the last half century, for the sharing of resources. This would require improvement of the bibliographic apparatus by which the existence of relevant materials is made known, and the improvement of arrangements for securing copies after identification. There exist precedents and prospective technology for both of these. However, an examination of the situation leads to the conclusion that the most useful development of all for the purpose of sharing might be the assignment of specific responsibility for certain conspicuous subjects to particular libraries, each of which would be obliged to acquire comprehensively in the subject, organize and publish its bibliography, and render a nationwide (or perhaps even international) backstopping lending or photocopy service in the subject.

There are many other aspects of the future of research libraries which have not been touched. Nothing has been said about their internal organization, or their physical arrangements, or about training for librarianship, or even about such important subjects as the improvement of the sources of cataloging information, and the sharing of the burden of acquisition through cooperative acquisitions projects. While some of these things relate more than others to the all-important matter of access, it is that to which most attention has been given. However, there remains one further consideration, not explicitly mentioned though implicit in all that has been said. If it is within the basic presumption of the general research library — and I believe it is — that the research use of library materials can and must play an increasingly important role for the conduct of human affairs, it follows that the research library of the future must increasingly find ways to promote and to facilitate such use. This will not be accomplished by inventing short-cuts in cataloging or book arrangement, or by discouraging interlibrary lending, or by shortchanging users because they do not appear to qualify in terms of scholarly achievement. The democratization of the library — the great achievement on which American librarianship should pride itself — need not result in diluted scholarship, but should result in greatly widened usefulness of these institutions wherein the experience of mankind is recorded. "Even the modern great library," said Dr. Bush in 1945 in the article to which I have previously referred, "is not generally consulted; it is nibbled at by a few." To librarians who are keenly aware of the wealth of potentially daily usefulness which is in their custody, but who realize from their own experience how inconvenient and frustrating it is to tap that wealth, this must be a challenge: How do we put the research library of the future to greater use? Some of the suggestions made here may contribute to that end; but there must be many more.

Appendix

The Problems of Research Libraries;
Programs for Solution

|

. . . .

The Problems
of the
General Research Libraries

The function of the research library is to make available, to the fullest extent of its assignment and its capabilities, the library materials needed by its constituency. While the specialized research library, concentrating upon a particular subject or period, can often limit its scope to its capacity for efficient service, the peculiar problem of the general research library (such as that of a university) arises from the gap that exists between what its users require and what it can supply. The principal causes of this discrepancy are the following:

A. *The gap between production and acquisition of library materials.* No library, no matter how well endowed with funds and collections, can acquire more than a fraction of what is produced. While the increasing diversification and intensification of research compel research libraries to acquire ever-larger quantities of materials, the worldwide acceleration in the production of these materials in all categories daily increases the gap between what a general research library desirably might and what it can acquire, organize, and hold.

B. *Obstacles to sharing resources.* Unable to meet all demands from its own collection, a research library should be able to augment its own resources by sharing those of other libraries. Arrangements have been developed for making this possible. Principal among these are cooperative acquisition programs, union catalogs, interlibrary lending, and photocopying services. All these perform yeoman's service. Yet the utmost to which these devices can provide access, even if they worked perfectly, would still be only the composite of the fractional collections of individual libraries. Meanwhile, the delays and frustrations which result from dependence upon these arrangements are so great that, except for occasional borrowings of extensive or very little-used materials, libraries much prefer local self-sufficiency and make every effort to achieve it.

C. *Bibliographic deficiencies.* Equally important with the obstacles which impede the research library's physical access to the library materials needed by its users are those which limit its knowledge of these materials. The whole purpose of a library is that it should be organized for use by bibliographic techniques; but because of the expense, no general research library can itself afford to perform more than a fraction of the bibliographic work by which even its own collections are organized for service. For the remainder of this bibliographic work it is dependent upon the central cataloging and classifying services

and upon published bibliographies, indexes, and catalogs. By the same token, its entire information regarding materials which are not in its own collection
is dependent upon bibliographic work performed by
others; and to the extent that this is deficient it is
ignorant. While it is true that there are thousands
of specialized bibliographical services, their very number and specialization are impediments in the sense
that no library can acquire them all nor can an inquirer often make profitable use of them. Meanwhile
there are great deficiencies in the comprehensive bibliographic tools which would immediately extend the
research library's reach: there is, for example, no
subject index to the National Union Catalog; the
extensive series of indexes published by the H. W.
Wilson Company covers only some 1,250 periodicals;
and the cataloging service of the Library of Congress
meets only approximately 50 per cent of the needs
of American university libraries.

D. *Inadequacy of techniques for physical maintenance,
record-keeping, and administration.* The principal
problems of the general research libraries can thus be
seen to stem from their need of prompt, assured, and
convenient access both in bibliographic and in physical terms to the world production of recorded knowledge. This need, typically commencing with the current domestic (national) production of books and
periodicals, extends in rapidly widening circles, corresponding with the ever-expanding interests of the
users, to other countries, languages, chronological
periods, and forms of material. But within the li-

brary the identical problems are repeated, in micro-
cosm, in terms of library management. Here again
are found the same requirements for prompt, assured,
and convenient access, both bibliographic and physical; these are made possible by the voluminous
record-keeping and the physical management which
is required for the building, the maintenance, the
organization, and the service of the collections. The
ultimate objective of all these activities is to assure
the identification and availability of a particular book
to satisfy a particular need. To achieve this purpose
an excellent body of practice has been developed
and, with limitations, is generally applied. But many
unsolved or imperfectly resolved problems reduce the
efficiency of the operation far below what is desired
or expected either by the users or the staff. Among
these problems in the areas of physical maintenance,
record-keeping, and in the mechanisms of management are the following:

1. *Problems of physical maintenance:* deterioration
   of book stock, high cost of adequate bookbinding,
   inefficient use of storage space, delays in delivery
   of books from the book stacks, difficulties of storage of nonbook materials, mutilation, and pilfer-
   ing.

2. *Problems of record-keeping:* high cost and inadequacies of the acquisition process (book selection,
   acquisitions-searching, procurement, etc.), high
   cost and inadequacies of cataloging, restrictions
   upon the availability of catalog information beyond the catalog room, high cost of updating the

catalog (e.g., to reflect changes in form of entry, holdings, or location of the materials), problems of organizing the collection for service to specialist groups, high cost and inefficiency of methods of recording serials, insufficiency of methods for recording books not on the shelf (including those charged out on loan), inadequacy of methods for guiding readers to appropriate sources of information, inadequacy of methods for enabling readers to copy extracts, etc.

3. *Problems of administration:* building design, testing and standardization of library equipment and supplies, securing information regarding available equipment and supplies, problems of local and regional organization for library service, inadequacy of statistical bases for planning for library work, difficulties of recruitment and training.

II
. . . .

Programs
of Research
for Overcoming the Obstacles

If the sources of the principal problems of the general research libraries have been correctly identified in the foregoing, it should be possible to design programs looking toward their solution. The previous discussion suggests the following 21 programs. They are described more particularly in Section III.

Improved self-sufficiency of resources

1. Development of the techniques of high-ratio-reduction microphotography as a means for promoting local self-sufficiency of resources

Improved arrangements for sharing resources

2. Improvement of the arrangements for sharing resources so as to approach more closely the efficiency of access provided by local ownership

Improved bibliographic access

3. Improvement of the supply of cataloging information
4. Improvement of the published bibliographic apparatus

5. Improvement of union catalogs

Improved methods of physical maintenance

6. Further attacks on the problem of deterioration of book stock

7. Improvements in methods and reduction of cost of bookbinding

8. Search for improved techniques of book storage

9. Search for improved techniques of book delivery from extensive storage areas

10. Improvement of methods and codification of information regarding the storage, preservation, and repair of library materials

11. Prevention of mutilation and pilferage

Improved methods of record-keeping (other than cataloging)

12. Improvement of the procedures of book acquisition

13. Improvement of record control of serials

14. Improvement of record control of circulation

15. Improvement of methods for directing readers

16. Improvement of methods for note-taking and copying

Improved bases of administration

17. Studies for improved building design

18. Standardization and testing of library equipment, supplies, and systems

19. Development of new or improved devices for library applications

20. Improvement of organization of library services

21. Recruitment and training for library work

III

. . . .

Details of Programs
for Overcoming
the Obstacles

PROGRAM 1. DEVELOPMENT OF THE TECHNIQUES
OF HIGH-RATIO-REDUCTION MICROPHOTOGRAPHY AS A
MEANS FOR PROMOTING LOCAL SELF-SUFFICIENCY
OF RESOURCES

Microphotography has made it possible for research
libraries to acquire important resources which would
otherwise have been denied to them because of cost or
scarcity. But microtext at present ratios of reduction is
still too expensive to permit the massive distribution of
less-used material which might constitute a major step
toward increasing the local self-sufficiency of general research libraries.

However, the techniques of high-ratio-reduction
microphotography, i.e., at a 100-diameter reduction and
more, which would permit the copying of many thousands of pages in the area required by a single original
page, offer the prospect of enabling the distribution of
large quantities of material at low cost and in very
compact form. At least four processes, and perhaps a

fifth, now are or are becoming available for this purpose. These are the Lippmann "grainless" emulsions (Eastman Kodak, Agfa, and others), Photochromic dyes (National Cash Register Company), the Philips mercury-diazonium process, the General Electric plastic recording process, and the Carson crystal color-center process.

Before a system can be based on any of the processes metioned above, a number of supporting techniques must be developed. The following are required:

a. The technique for miniaturizing original records by the particular process selected, in such a manner as to take advantage of the high resolution offered by the process so as not to lose any of the information contained in the original, allowing for the interposition of one or more generation of copies either in the production and multifolding of the miniaturized image or in its exploitation.

b. The techniques for bibliographic identification of the miniaturized material, providing its "address" in the miniaturized store. (For example, suppose that the *Congressional Record* were miniaturized at high reduction. A search of the *Record* ordinarily involves a search of one or more of the multiple indexes contained in one or more of the final volumes of the set for each session of Congress. It is very easy to locate these indexes in a set of the original volumes displayed on shelves. It becomes much more difficult to do so if the indexes must first be identified in a bibliography and then hunted out by "address" from a miniaturized store. Such problems must be foreseen and solutions provided.)

c. The techniques for locating desired images in the store and for displaying them visually. (Involved here is a queuing problem: if one person is using the indexes to the *Congressional Record* for the 2nd Session of the 84th Congress, will it be possible for another person simultaneously to consult the indexes for the 1st Session?)

d. The techniques for providing "hard copy" as needed.

e. The techniques for protecting the store against damage and loss in use.

To the above, which are principally engineering problems, might be added the following, which is of a different character:

f. The development of arrangements by which copyrighted material may be included in such a miniaturized library without losing the advantage of price reduction which such miniaturization offers.

It is obvious that each of the above poses a difficult problem, the solution of which will require much ingenuity.

At the present time the only approximation to a system of this kind is the Verac, of which a working model has been constructed by the AVCO Corporation with assistance from the Council on Library Resources.[1] In

. . . .

[1] K. Bowker, L. H. Martin, E. J. Lucas, and C. Phaneuf, *Technical Investigation of Elements of a Mechanized Library System, Final Report No. EW-6680* (Boston: Electronics Research Laboratories, Crosley Division, Avco Corporation, 1960); R. L. Waring, *Technical Investigations of Addition of a Hard-*

this engine the photostore consists of a stack of plates on which images of textual material are recorded on Lippmann emulsion at a 140-diameter reduction, making use of a precision camera constructed for the purpose. The store, approximately a cubic foot in dimension, is designed to hold a million images. To find a desired image, the address of the specific plate, column, and row at which the image is located must be known. When this address is signaled to the machine, a servo-mechanism brings the addressed image into the scanning position through a paroxysmic effort of approximately one-tenth of a second's duration. In this position the image may be projected optically and enlarged on 16- or 35-millimeter microfilm, which, after processing, furnishes "hard copy" in a form which itself represents a considerable reduction from the size of the original. However, the image in this position may alternatively be scanned by a vidicon (television camera), and the resulting signal can create a display on a television screen. If at this point it should be necessary to consult the store in another search, the image can be transferred to a memory tube so as to enable the television display to persist for the use of the first inquirer while freeing the store for the second. Finally, the signal from the vidicon can be (and is currently) fed to a Printapix tube, resulting in the almost instantaneous production of "hard copy" in the full size of the original.

. . . .

copy Output to the Elements of a Mechanized Library System. Final Report 940101 (Cincinnati, Ohio: Electronics and Ordnance Division, Avco Corporation, 1961); Council on Library Resources, *Annual Report* 4:29-30 (1961); 5:25-28 (1962).

(The Printapix tube is a cathode ray tube designed by Litton Industries for electrostatic printing. In response to signals received from the vidicon as it scans the miniaturized image, the tube transmits electrostatic charges, through metallic elements embedded in its face, to paper moving across its face at a speed of 33 inches per minute. These metallic elements are actually fine wires, .001 inches in diameter, set .003 inches on centers. The electrostatic image thus created on the paper is developed by processes which have become familiar in electrostatic reproduction. The entire process, from the signal initiating the retrieval process to the completion of the "hard copy," takes about two seconds. The resolution of the "hard copy" is controlled by (a) the resolution of the miniaturized image, (b) the resolution of the vidicon, and (c) the resolution of the Printapix and the associated development of the electrostatic image. Since the metallic conductors of the Printapix are set .003 inches on centers, the tube itself is capable of a resolution of 333 lines per inch (13 lines per millimeter), which may be considered adequate for all textual and much other library material.)

It is obvious that this mechanism represents a very considerable engineering achievement, and one that is easily capable of still further refinement. The question is whether it is worth such refinement. To answer this question the economics of the system must be examined.

Let it be supposed that the mechanism could be purchased for $100,000, to be amortized over ten years; that the cost of maintenance were $1,000 a year; that the cost of materials (film, paper, toner, etc.) were $20 per 1,000 pages (film or paper); and that a miniaturized library of a million pages could be procured at the cost of .0075¢ per page, or $75.

At 20,000 pages per annum (10 per hour) the per-page cost of "hard copy" would be 57¢. At 40,000 pages a year (20 per hour) the per-page cost would drop to 30¢. In order to get into the range of 10¢ per page the load would have to be 137,500 pages per year, or approximately one page per minute, 8 hours a day, 300 days a year.

(If the use of the device were limited to viewing desired images on television screens, without provision for "hard copy," the per-page cost would be approximately the same, since the controlling factor is the $10,000 a year amortization charge on the device.)

It is apparent from the above that the cost of the mechanism will have destroyed what was the initial intention of the development, namely the inexpensive dissemination of library materials. For even at 10¢ per page few persons would be willing to procure more than an occasional 10-page article; a 300-page book would be for practical purposes out of the question.

The Verac may, in consequence, be said to have demonstrated several things: that it is possible to mechanize a store of library materials at high reduction ratios and to retrieve desired images for consultation or in "hard copy" very rapidly and in a form adequate for use; but that the cost of the mechanism must be brought down much below that of this particular device if the advantages offered by high-ratio microreduction are to be exploited.

These advantages are, however, so attractive (and indeed essential) as to demand that further efforts be made to exploit them. Experience to date indicates that these must be along the lines of finding comparatively simple and inexpensive methods for meeting the technical requirements set out above.

PROGRAM 2. IMPROVEMENT OF THE ARRANGEMENTS FOR SHARING RESOURCES SO AS TO APPROACH MORE CLOSELY THE EFFICIENCY OF ACCESS PROVIDED BY LOCAL OWNERSHIP

Present arrangements for sharing resources, based upon cooperative acquisitions programs, union catalog projects, interlibrary lending and photocopying services, have about reached the ultimate of which they are capable on their present bases of voluntary cooperation and interinstitutional courtesy which must always defer to the prior claims of local clienteles.

Sharing of resources involves two elements: knowledge of the location of needed material, and the ability to obtain it from that location, either in original or in photocopy.

If sharing resources is genuinely to compete with local ownership and not to remain (as it is now) a form of dependency to be avoided, it is obvious that improvements in both of these elements are required. Information regarding the location of needed material should be obtainable much more simply than now; and in the arrangements for obtaining loans of photocopies there must be improvements with respect to certainty, promptness, and reduction of present costs, caused to a considerable degree by the formalities (paper work) involved.

With respect to the first of these elements, although union catalogs and lists are not the only means for locating needed materials, they nevertheless stand among the most important devices for this purpose, and sooner or later any arrangement for sharing of resources, whether local, regional, or national, requires — for anything approaching real effectiveness — tools of these kinds. Their improvement is the subject of Program 5.

With respect to the other particulars in which improvement is needed, it is apparent that these are in general involved in the relationship of the requested to the requesting library, and the degree of the responsibility for services of the former to the latter. It may be concluded from the present situation that any major improvement must be based not upon courtesy arrangements but upon specific assignments of responsibility, accompanied by funds to enable the assignments to be executed. This principle is being adopted in a number of programs for the improvement of statewide library services which contemplate the appropriation of funds to certain libraries in return for making their collections available to other libraries in the state.

Accordingly, it would appear that any program for the improvement of the conditions for sharing of resources should aim at finding bases for assignments of specific responsibility for the services which make such sharing a reality. It is possible, too, that certain technological improvements, such as telefacsimile, may be brought to the work; but the major defects in the present system appear to be administrative rather than technological.

In this connection, attention may be drawn to an interesting example, at the national level, of a library whose assigned (statutory) responsibility contemplates not a local but — at the very least — a national clientele. This is the National Library of Medicine. This library provides a service for the literature of medicine complementing but not supplanting that of other libraries. Because of the comprehensiveness of the collections of this library, it is only occasionally necessary to turn to any other library in the United States for material in this subject, once the local resources have been exhausted. Union catalogs and lists are similarly to a degree rendered unnecessary in this field of literature; for most titles it may be assumed that, if they fall within this subject, they may be found in this particular library. Furthermore, this library publishes the principal current bibliography of the subject; and since this bibliography is based on its own collections, it is a catalog of them, simplifying still further the access to materials.

In Great Britain a somewhat similar situation exists with respect to the National Lending Library for Science and Technology. This library, which has taken over the back files of periodicals from the Science Library (South Kensington), has been established by the Department of Industrial and Scientific Research at Boston Spa, Yorkshire, where it exists for the sole purpose of supplementing local resources in scientific and technological literature through interlibrary loans and photocopying services.

The services of these two libraries do not constitute "sharing of resources" in the usual sense. Rather, they are additional services provided by the national governments to reinforce the resources of local institutions. Whereas with most libraries the interlibrary services are subordinated to the needs of the local constituencies, in the case of these libraries the interlibrary service has a primary claim.

If services such as these were available for all, or for even a number of principal, subjects of inquiry, it may be doubted whether many libraries would feel the need for local self-sufficiency as strongly as they do now. However, it would appear that a prerequisite for a satisfactory service of this kind must be a clear assignment of responsibility whether by subject or some other categorization, so that an inquiring library may turn with confidence to that agency which can complement its local resources in a particular category, without having to go through a locating mechanism such as a union catalog.

It is possible that, with effort, such arrangements could be extended in the United States in a number of subjects in addition to medicine. Agriculture, law, and chemistry immediately suggest themselves. There are certainly others.

The first step toward the execution of such a program would be to evaluate the present usual arrangements for sharing resources against the special arrangements in this country with respect to medicine and in Great Britain with respect to scientific and technological literature with a view to ascertaining the actual experience and needs

of libraries and their users, comparative costs, bibliographical, legal, and financial bases of operation, etc., as
a preliminary to planning further action.

PROGRAM 3. IMPROVEMENT OF THE SUPPLY
OF CATALOGING INFORMATION

The principal means of access to the contents of the
collections of a general research library are of two kinds:
the bibliographical apparatus which it constructs itself,
and that which it purchases ready-made from publishers.
The latter consists of the bibliographies, indexes, and
abstracting services without which much of its collections
would remain a closed book, but which are prepared
almost entirely without any effort or control on its part.

The essential bibliographic apparatus which the library must itself create in order to provide its users with
access to its collections consists principally of its own
catalog and — ordinarily in American libraries — the
systematic arrangement of its books on the shelves, reflected by its shelf list.

For the construction of even this apparatus the library
cannot claim full credit. Typically, much of the cataloging of the individual works in its collection is performed by central cataloging services, of which those of
the Library of Congress are the most important and best
known; the cataloging and filing rules which it follows
are typically the result of joint enterprise; and the book
classification which it uses for its shelf arrangement is
maintained and even applied to individual works by
central services.

In spite of all this assistance, the maintenance of the apparatus is not only costly, but in other ways falls short of satisfaction. The cost ($5 per title is not unusual or even the maximum, taking together all titles both old and new, in English and in foreign languages, those with and those without Library of Congress catalog cards) reflects to a degree the difficulty of procuring cataloging information from central sources when needed; it reflects, too, the difficulties of catalog maintenance, including its updating to show changes of entry, holdings, or location, and to avoid congestion. Other problems concern the uniformity of cataloging practice, adequacy of central-service cataloging, and the making of catalog information available beyond the catalog room (e.g., in branch libraries or professors' offices).

It is not easy to improve the cataloging problem or to lessen its expense. Over-all studies are needed to identify possible areas of improvement. The following specific programs of study deserve investigation:

a. *Improvement of supply of cataloging information from central services.* At least two investigations suggest themselves under this head.

   i. *Increased coverage of cataloging information.* The cataloging costs of an individual library can be reduced to the extent that it can use the cataloging information prepared by others. In typical American research library practice, this means the use of Library of Congress cards. But these cards have been found to provide university libraries with only 50 to 60 per cent of needed information. Large sums could be saved to such libraries if even another 10 per cent of their books could be cataloged with the use of information from central sources. (For example, if fifty libraries could save $2.50 on each of an additional thousand books per year, representing a total of 5,000 different titles, the annual saving would be $125,000, while the cost of cataloging these books might not exceed $25,000.) Within recent months the Library of Congress has commenced the issuance of proof sheets representing catalog cards prepared by libraries other than itself. This marks a forward step. Can it be extended? A next step in exploring the question would be an investigation of methods by which cataloging information useful to a group of libraries might be generated and distributed.

ii. *A limited "cataloging in source" program.* Although a general "cataloging in source" program was not found feasible by the Library of Congress in its 1960 report,[2] it is quite possible that a limited program (perhaps restricted to a particular area of costly-to-catalog publications, such as certain government documents) might be found to be useful, and should be investigated.

b. *Uniformity in cataloging.*

i. *Under ALA rules.* Uniformity in cataloging is not easy to attain. It is not unknown for four principal research libraries, following identical cataloging

. . . .
[2] U.S. Library of Congress, Processing Department, *The Cataloging-in-Source Experiment. A Report to the Librarian of Congress by the Director of the Processing Department* (Washington, D.C.: Library of Congress, 1960).

rules, to catalog the same current English-language trade book under four different entries. (The situation may be expected to be aggravated with respect to foreign-language titles.) The obvious corrective of this situation is prompter availability of central-service cataloging. An investigation of the methods for effecting this could be conducted simultaneously as part of the inquiry suggested under a, i, above.

ii. *Consistency of rules.* However, there is another aspect of the situation with respect to uniformity in cataloging. In recent years, with the development of the extensive bibliographic activities of a number of federal government agencies (the Atomic Energy Commission, the Armed Services Technical Information Agency [now the Department of Defense Documentation Center], the Office of Technical Service of the Department of Commerce, and the National Aeronautics and Space Agency), there have grown up cataloging practices affecting the so-called "technical report" literature which are inconsistent with the ALA *Rules* followed by American libraries generally. As a result, not only will identical reports be found under different entries in the bibliographies published by these agencies (and the catalogs of the special libraries which follow their practice) from those under which they would be found in most libraries, but when any of these reports are to be incorporated into the collections of a library using the ALA *Rules* they must be recataloged, although already cataloged by one of the agencies named. This is needless inconsistency and waste. An effort should be launched to eliminate the inconsistency before it goes even further than it has.

c. *Adequacy of cataloging.* The adequacy of the cataloging provided by the central cataloging services has never been seriously studied in its relation to the adequacy of the local cataloging which depends upon them. If it is the function of the library to make its collections useful, the adequacy of the cataloging is a principal factor involved. At the present time many periodicals are much better analyzed than are any books. An inquiry is needed.

d. *Catalog organization and maintenance.* No matter what cataloging information is available from central services, the organization and maintenance of the catalog is exclusively a local responsibility. It is laborious and expensive. Studies in cataloging are likely to concern themselves with the individual entry; the catalog needs to be studied holistically as well. Two such studies may be suggested.

i. *Methods of updating the catalog.* Attention needs to be given to the problem of how to organize the catalog so that it can be efficiently updated (e.g., to reflect changes in location, additions to holdings, etc.). Present practices are cumbersome. A study is required to ascertain less expensive practices, either with respect to catalogs as now organized, or by so organizing the catalog as to make it more susceptible to such changes.

ii. *Chronological cutoff.* As the catalog grows, reflecting a continuously increasing proportion of older material, it becomes desirable to make a cutoff based on chronology and to start anew. But the known disadvantages of multiple catalogs are so great and the advantage of a single catalog so clear as to deter such action. A study is needed to ascertain how the advantages can be gained with avoidance of disadvantages.

e. *Dissemination of the catalog.* In many situations (e.g., university campuses, public library systems) it is desirable to make the information contained in the catalog available beyond the catalog room of the main library. There are a number of precedents for this: certain great libraries have published their catalogs; several state and public library systems employ punched-card tabulating equipment to publish catalogs for the use of their branches. None of these systems as yet quite provides the equivalent of the central catalog; also, the expense of such publication does not permit general adoption. It is quite possible, however, that automatic methods (e.g., sequential cameras or computers) can be successfully applied to this problem. A survey of needed equipment and procedures is desirable.

f. *Providing cataloging information for specialist groups.* This is a variation of the problem of dissemination of the catalog beyond the main catalog room. Specialist groups within a larger group frequently require a segregation from the main catalog of the information pertaining to their interests. It should be possible to effect such segregation by nearly automatic procedures. A study is desirable looking to the improvement of techniques available for this purpose.

g. *Alternative forms of the catalog.* While the traditional card catalog continues to perform yeoman's service, it is apparent that from some points of view (e.g., updating, dissemination) it is inflexible and costly. In recent years new devices and techniques of cataloging have been developed which lend themselves much better to the use of automata. These have hardly been considered with respect to their application to the needs of large general research libraries. Such consideration might lead to the development of techniques more suitable for their use than those now employed.

h. *Automation and the catalog.* It is quite possible, as suggested in several of the foregoing paragraphs, that a number of the problems of the catalog could be solved through the introduction of automata or other mechanisms at various points in the cataloging process. Indeed, just as the card catalog, making use of unit cards distributed from a central source, itself represented the results of mechanical advances, so in recent years cataloging has benefited from some of the newer technological developments — photo-offset lithography, punched-card electrical accounting machines, and sequential cameras. The impending availability of computer-controlled typesetting systems commanding the wide variety of type sorts required for bibliographic purposes offers possibilities of major improvements. A study of the means for realizing these possibilities will soon be urgent.

i. *Special devices.* A number of special devices needed
for the processes of cataloging are listed in Program 19.

PROGRAM 4. IMPROVEMENT OF THE PUBLISHED
BIBLIOGRAPHIC APPARATUS

In the discussion of the previous program attention
was called to the fact that an important part of the
bibliographic apparatus which provides access to the
collections of a research library consists of the bibliographies, indexes, and abstracting services which the
library purchases ready-made from publishers. Lacking
this apparatus, much of its collections — specifically its
collections of periodical and journal literature, government documents, and much other material besides
(essays, reviews, law reports, "technical" reports, etc.)
— would remain a closed book. In any one year, many
more entries which refer to the library's collections are
added to the published bibliographic apparatus than are
added by the library itself to its own catalog.

Several comments may be made regarding this situation. The first is that, except in a few exceptional in-
stances, the library and the library world exercise prac-
tically no control over the conditions which affect the
compilation and publication of this apparatus. Libraries
pay a large portion of the bill, but are only infrequently
consulted as to the content, arrangement, or other
aspects of these publications.

A second comment is that the published bibliographic
apparatus, as a whole, does not constitute a recognizable

system. The variations from one bibliographic service to another — in scope, coverage, arrangement, periodicity, format, etc. — are so great that they create a confusing welter rather than a perspicuous guide to published information. The International Federation for Documentation has listed many thousands of indexing and abstracting services in the natural and social sciences alone;[3] the very number of these services prohibits any single library from securing all of them and would deter an inquirer from making use of all of them even were they available. As a result, inquirers tend to avoid, as much as they can, recourse to apparatus which is only too likely to result in any case in the discovery of references to material not locally available, and to limit their inquiries as much as possible to the library's own catalog or shelves.[4] A too frequent consequence of such avoidance is bibliographic ignorance which is all too common in those from whom a familiarity with the bibliographical tools of their subject might be expected.

Librarians have endlessly discussed the defects of the published bibliographical apparatus and have established committees at national and international levels and conducted institutes and meetings to deal with the problems. These have had little effect. Many of the principal bibliographic services are controlled by the professional associations for the various disciplines which are rarely

. . . .

[3] *Index Bibliographicus,* 4th ed. (The Hague: International Federation for Documentation, 1959 —).

[4] Of course, such avoidance is not always possible: for law, medicine, chemistry, physics, language and literature studies, and general periodical literature, recourse to the published bibliographic apparatus is unavoidable and normal.

moved by the exhortations of librarians. In the natural sciences the abstract, invented to provide "current awareness," has become a sacred cow of bibliographic analysis, even though for the most part its utility for its original purpose may be suspected to be long since diminished, and even though its continued use results in intolerable delays and costliness of publication. But governments have in recent years been persuaded to share these costs, while to compensate for the delays a new form of bibliography, the "permuted index," compiled by computers, has been introduced, adding still further to the cost.

Perhaps a new examination of this situation would be useful, if made from the point of view of the institutions (the general research libraries) which contribute so much to the support of these services through their purchase of them, which bind, keep, and service them, and which more than most have the opportunity to observe how they are used or neglected. Such an examination should look to improvement, both with respect to the details of individual publications (scope, coverage, arrangement, promptness, duplicativeness, cost, serviceability to users, etc.) and with a view to promoting the development of a perspicuous system to which the individual publications would contribute.

PROGRAM 5. IMPROVEMENT OF UNION CATALOGS

A prerequisite to the physical sharing of resources is bibliographic access to them. Among the principal tools for such bibliographic access are the national and regional union catalogs and lists. To the extent that these are deficient, sharing of resources is impeded.

The greatest of such catalogs is the National Union Catalog at the Library of Congress, constructed by the cooperative efforts of hundreds of research libraries with private and governmental assistance. This catalog, which records some 13,000,000 separate titles published before 1956, is in the first place incomplete as a record of holdings of American research libraries. In the second place, it is exclusively an "author catalog" and provides no access by subject. In the third place, it is available only in Washington.

If this catalog could be completed with respect to its record of holdings, amplified with respect to subject cataloging, and finally made easily available to users outside of Washington, the resources of every research library would be instantly and enormously extended and the requirements for local self-sufficiency might be correspondingly reduced.

It would not be easy or inexpensive to accomplish these objectives. A first step would consist in a feasibility study.

Publications post-1956 which are reported by participating libraries to the National Union Catalog are listed by the Library of Congress in a cumulative monthly publication entitled *The National Union Catalog of Books.* This, like the National Union Catalog on cards, is an "author catalog." Again, it is desirable that subject access be provided. This is a continuing service, supported by sales, and it would be difficult to devise the mechanism for providing the subject access within the available support. However, the possibilities should be explored.

In addition to the needed projects described above, there is great need for improving the technology of creating, maintaining, and consulting union catalogs. It is obvious that these tools are essential for the sharing of resources, whether on a national, regional, or state basis; they can also be of great use in reducing the local costs of cataloging, in assisting book selection, and in bibliographic work. But for these purposes it is necessary that they be maintained up to date and that the service from them be prompt and otherwise efficient. Because of the size of these catalogs and the number of participants, present techniques have broken down. (It it for this reason that the Library of Congress now publishes the list of post-1956 books reported to the National Union Catalog.) New techniques need to be developed and a study should be initiated.

PROGRAM 6. FURTHER ATTACKS ON THE PROBLEM OF DETERIORATION OF BOOK STOCK

From the investigations of W. J. Barrow[5] it is now known that few of the books printed in the first half of this century can be expected to be of much use by its end. The problem of deterioration which is thus presented must be met on two fronts — by rescuing the books of the chemical-wood paper period (roughly from 1870 to the present), and by promoting the use of

. . . .
[5] W. J. Barrow and R. C. Sproull, "Permanence in Book Papers," *Science* 129:1075-84 (April 24, 1959).

permanent/durable papers for the future. Several programs are already under way for these purposes; others
are needed.

a. *Aerosol deacidification.* Mr. Barrow is working on a
process for the deacidification of books by an aerosol
spray.[6] It is hoped that this process may not only be
effective but also sufficiently inexpensive that it may
be adopted for application in libraries. However,
even if successful, the process cannot restore lost
strength; it can only delay deterioration. Furthermore, many of the books to which it might be applied
will already be beyond help. Other and more per-
manently effective means of rescue are needed.

b. *Preservation by photography.* The Association of Research Libraries has undertaken a study of the magnitude of the required rescue operation and of the
methods and cost of executing it.[7] It is likely that
the preservative medium will be photographic. By
present methods this will prove enormously expensive.
Methods for reducing the cost must be sought. It is
obvious that a rescue operation of this kind could be
combined with a program for disseminating resources
as described in Program 1, and the techniques of
high-ratio-reduction photography, which could be
similarly applied, should be studied in this connection.

. . . .

[6] Council on Library Resources, *Annual Report* 6:22 (1961).
[7] Council on Library Resources, *Annual Report* 6:22 (1961);
E. E. Williams, "Magnitude of the Paper-Deterioration Problem
as Measured by a National Union Catalog Sample," *College &
Research Libraries* 23:499, 543 (November, 1962).

c. *Permanent/durable paper.* As a result of the studies conducted with the support of the Council on Library Resources, Mr. Barrow has developed specifications and a formula for producing a permanent/durable book paper within economic feasibilities. A number of manufacturers are producing such papers, but there is no present method for validating claims or assuring adherence to specifications. Consequently, the American Library Association has established a consumer-industry committee to promote the use of permanent/durable paper in books for the library market.[8] It is foreseeable that the work of this committee should be supported by funds for testing and possibly also for further research.

d. *The thermodynamics of the cellulose molecule.* The solutions to the deterioration problem described in the three previous paragraphs are all technological in nature. It is, however, continually apparent that there are large gaps in our scientific knowledge regarding the behavior of paper and other cellulose products, and that basic research is required. The National Bureau of Standards has suggested the desirability of a study in the thermodynamics of the cellulose molecule. Such basic studies, if prosecuted over a period of time, might result in knowledge leading to fundamental alterations in paper manufacture and storage, book binding, etc.

. . . .
[8] V. W. Clapp, " 'Permanent/Durable' Book Papers," *ALA Bulletin* 57:847-852 (October, 1963).

PROGRAM 7. IMPROVEMENTS IN METHODS AND
REDUCTION OF COST OF BOOKBINDING

For most books in most American libraries hand sewing is a thing of the past, due to the expense resulting
from the high labor cost. As a result, methods of machine sewing are used which do not permit books to
open properly. In the very home of the book the inmates
are maimed and crippled — a situation intolerable not
only aesthetically but also technologically, because these
methods of binding interfere both with the use of the
books and with their rebinding when that becomes
necessary.

"Perfect" (also known as "adhesive") binding would
seem to provide a solution. In this form of bookbinding
the leaves are no longer sewn through the folds, but are
trimmed at the binding edge and held together by a
flexible adhesive. Should the adhesive fail, however, the
book falls apart in separate leaves. Accordingly, because of the lack of demonstrated prospect of permanence of the adhesive, such binding is currently unac-
ceptable for use in research libraries.

In this situation it becomes important to develop a
predictably permanent adhesive. But at the moment
there is no sure way of predicting the permanence of an
adhesive. Furthermore, library books (especially periodicals) are often composed of papers of varying character,
with very differing requirements for adhesives.

Mr. W. J. Barrow is at present engaged in a program
for devising methods of predicting the permanence of
adhesives and their suitability to library bookbinding.[9]
. . . .

[9] Council on Library Resources, *Annual Report* 6:22 (1961).

In the nature of the case this is a slow process. Because the stakes are large it is desirable to speed up the program — the annual library bookbinding bill runs into millions of dollars. If a satisfactory method of "perfect" binding could be developed it would not only improve the product but reduce the cost.

Further steps that might be taken:

a. To employ several laboratories in parallel experimentation directed toward the identification of suitable adhesives for "perfect" binding.

b. To conduct basic research on paper and adhesives, such as is suggested under Program 6, with the hope of finding the clue to permanent flexibility and adhesion of materials which combine in a bookbinding.

c. To investigate the possibility of developing a machine which will effect, for library job-binding, the result of hand sewing (as the Smythe machine does for edition binding).

PROGRAM 8. SEARCH FOR IMPROVED TECHNIQUES OF BOOK STORAGE

As a library's collections outgrow the space provided for them, a choice must be made for relieving the pressure, whether by providing expanded storage space, by draining off the less-used books into a nearby storage warehouse or to a cooperative storage warehouse at a greater distance, by abandoning the shelf classification of the collection and shelving them compactly, etc.

This problem has not remained unstudied. The University of Chicago has developed a formula for predicting the use of books with a view to allocating space on an expectancy-of-use basis.[10] Yale is identifying criteria for assigning books to compact storage and is studying ways to compensate for their removal from the open shelves.[11] A study at the Library of Congress proposed to design a method for evaluating the utility of the shelf classification with its costly use of storage space.[12] Still another study at Rutgers recently explored the economics of cooperative warehouses.[13]

Much further study is needed. What is the optimum size of an open-access collection? Do the alternatives to the classified collection provide compensatory advantages? What is the best method of management of a storage collection? How can the records of a storage warehouse collection be integrated with those of the regular collection? These and other questions need to be explored, and the results need to be put together in a guide to practice.

PROGRAM 9. SEARCH FOR IMPROVED TECHNIQUES OF BOOK DELIVERY FROM EXTENSIVE STORAGE AREAS

The book conveyor (mechanical or, more recently,

. . . .

[10] H. H. Fussler and J. L. Simon, *Patterns in the Use of Books in Large Research Libraries* (The University of Chicago Library, 1961).

[11] J. H. Ottemiller and others, "The Selective Book Retirement Program at Yale," *The Yale University Library Gazette* 34:64-72 (October, 1959).

[12] H. J. Dubester, "Stack Use of a Research Library," *ALA Bulletin* 53:891-893 (November, 1961).

[13] H. J. Harrar, *Cooperative Storage Warehouses* (graduate thesis, Rutgers University, New Brunswick, N.J., 1962).

pneumatic) has been a familiar instrument in book stacks since the end of the nineteenth century. Even with its assistance, book delivery in large collections is frequently excessively dilatory. While great advances in materials-handling have been made for other purposes, they have not reached libraries.

It is possible that any improvement in the handling of books in book stacks may involve not only the method of conveyance but the design of the book stacks. In view of the fact that the collections of research libraries are increasing rapidly, studies of this problem should be initiated at an early date in order to assure that no available improvements are missed.

It is possible that studies under this head might be profitably consolidated with those suggested under Program 8.

Program 10. Improvement of Methods
and Codification of Information Regarding the
Storage, Preservation, and Repair
of Library Materials

The collections of a large general research library include not only books, pamphlets, periodicals, and newspapers, but many kinds of nonbook materials — manuscripts, maps, music, prints and posters, sound recordings on discs and tape, microtexts on film and in several other forms, motion pictures, even punched cards and computer tape, with perhaps a scattering of cuneiform tablets, papyrus fragments, and parchment scrolls.

There is at present little to provide guidance to best

practice for housing and preservation of these various materials. How should a collection of posters best be kept? What are the optimum arrangements for manuscripts in the form of personal papers? What is the best treatment to accord a disintegrating seventeenth-century book still in original binding? What are the best temperature and humidity levels for a storage library? What are the best measures for protecting books in tropical climates?

Much information exists on all of these topics. Much of it is traditional and should be superseded. A manual of practice needs to be developed, bringing together the information which is now scattered, weeding out the superseded practice, developing new techniques or devices where needed, and pointing out gaps in knowledge.

PROGRAM 11. PREVENTION OF MUTILATION
AND PILFERAGE

Mutilation and pilferage is a serious problem in many general research libraries. Temporary secretion of books to serve private ends is an ancient problem in educational libraries, but actual theft has risen in recent years until it is calculated in a number of libraries at several per cent of the entire book stock each year. The amount of loss due to mutilation is unknown but in many institutions is conceded to be serious.

There is, of course, no single solution to this problem. Supervision of reading rooms and book stacks, guarding of entrances, the moral climate — all have their effect.

So also do access to inexpensive copying devices, and the availability of multiple copies.

Various proposals have been made for prevention of theft — pass systems, the use of magnetic or radioactive tracers, even odors. A firm in Columbus, Ohio (Storgard) has devised a clever system for preventing pilferage in stores, factories, motels, and elsewhere, but this does not appear to be foolproof against undergraduates.

Since it is not likely that any single solution to these problems will be found, a possible best step would be to institute a series of studies directed at ascertaining the facts in relation to the various physical and sociological circumstances. Such studies might at least sharpen up the problem, bring together the evidences of present best practice, and perhaps point the way to further profitable investigation.

PROGRAM 12. IMPROVEMENT OF THE PROCEDURES
OF BOOK ACQUISITION

The acquisitions process is a complex of operations involving many separate procedures, devices, and bibliographical tools. Improvements are possible at many points and of many different kinds. They can be as simple as the introduction of the multiple order form, or as complicated as the development of the Latin American Cooperative Acquisitions Project.

A recent attempt to improve the process hoped to involve the cooperation of publishers in so coding their books that not only might books be ordered by code, but that the code would itself indicate certain essential facts regarding the books. The hope was based upon the prospect that publishers would need to code their books in any case in order to permit computer handling of their accounts. In the event, this prospect faded, and with it the hope.[14]

Another interesting possibility which has been proposed concerns the simplification of the "acquisitions-searching" process (i.e., the checking to ascertain whether or not a book is already owned) by assigning a computer to the task; but much preparatory work is required before this can become an actuality.

In an area of activity such as acquisitions work, demanding improvements all along the line but not providing clear indications of developments which would provide the greatest assistance, it would seem desirable to institute a study of the entire process with a view to identifying the areas most needing and most susceptible to improvement.

PROGRAM 13. IMPROVEMENT OF RECORD CONTROL
OF SERIALS

Serials (periodicals and other sequential publications) which have been estimated to constitute 75 per cent of all products of the printing press, form not only a very important but also an increasingly large proportion of the acquisitions of research libraries. Their management is, however, costly. A principal part of this cost is in
....

[14] G. A. Harrar and A. Ladenson, "A Proposal for a National Code Number System for Current Publications," *Library Resources & Technical Services* 6:4-12 (Winter, 1962).

record-keeping, which includes checking in and routing separate issues as received, differentiating between copies, keeping track of missing issues and claiming them betimes, assuring the completion of volumes with title pages and indexes, scheduling completed volumes for the bindery, recording the bound volumes, paying for and renewing subscriptions. If, as is desirable, the receipt of issues is also announced to the library's users, this constitutes still another task. The matter is complicated by irregularities and delays in publication and receipt of issues, changes in title and format, linguistic and other difficulties in recognizing the identifying data in the publications, etc.

The devices and procedures now used for this record-keeping are still, in spite of manifold efforts at improvement, very labor-consuming. (The Library of Congress, for example, which processes some 1.8 million serial issues per year, employs forty or more persons in its Serial Record Division.)

This is, in consequence, an activity which calls aloud for the application of automata. Several attempts have made some progress in this direction.[15] The complexity of the problem is exemplified by the fact that one of these attempts has developed a computer program, based on only 100 serial titles, which has generated no fewer

· · · · · · · ·

[15] Estelle Brodman, "Mechanization of Library Procedures in the Medium-Sized Medical Library," *Bulletin of the Medical Library Association* 51:313-338 (July, 1963); Council on Library Resources, *University of California at San Diego to Continue Inquiry into Computerization of Serial Records . . . (Recent Developments, no. 87)* (Washington, D.C., 1962).

than 2,300 computer program instructions. This method of attack should be continued.

PROGRAM 14. IMPROVEMENT OF RECORD CONTROL
OF CIRCULATION

The whole elaborate labor of the research library is stultified when a book which is recorded as being in its collections cannot be produced at demand. Yet this occurrence happens with increasing frequency as the size of the library and the number of its users increase. On these occasions the only acceptable explanation is that the book is in process or in use, that the location is known, and that it can be produced in reasonable time.

Yet the means of record-keeping to support such an explanation, to facilitate prompt report to the user, and to obviate his frustration and vexation are very imperfect and so costly that they are ordinarily applied to only a part of the library's total circulation. There is ordinarily a record of books on loan outside the building, another of books in the bindery, and one of those assigned to cubicles, seminar rooms, and the reserve collection; but ordinarily not one for books in use in the reading room.

The Library Technology Project of the American Library Association has sponsored an elaborate comparison of the effectiveness of various charging systems which resulted in the publication in 1961 of a manual on the subject.[16] Since then, a number of research libraries,

. . . .

[16] George Fry & Associates, Inc., *Study of Circulation Control Systems, Public Libraries, College and University Libraries,*

including Brooklyn College, the University of California at Los Angeles, and Harvard, have adopted circulation systems based on punched-card electrical accounting machine equipment. Others, including Princeton and the City College of New York, have adopted systems based upon readers' embossed identification cards. At least one, Southern Illinois University, is using a computer in preparing a new circulation system. It is apparent that the most effective system is still to be devised, and that more work is needed.

Meanwhile, the general problem of internal record-keeping with respect to the location of books has not been touched. The possibilities of automatic recording have been suggested but have not been investigated. A feasibility study is in order.

PROGRAM 15. IMPROVEMENT OF METHODS
FOR DIRECTING READERS

Because the catalog is too detailed to serve as a general guide to sources of information in response to inquiries as formulated by users, libraries ordinarily provide a reference service, staffed by persons capable of intermediating between the users, the catalog, and the collections. Libraries of educational institutions usually also attempt to provide some kind of formal instruction in the use of the library. Because of the existence of these services, the development of other means of guidance is ordinarily neglected in libraries. In few general research libraries
. . . .
Special Libraries (Chicago: Library Technology Project, American Library Association, 1961).

is it possible for a stranger, even though he be informed regarding sources of information, to find his way directly from the vestibule to that part of the library where he may be best served. Similarly a student needs, when the occasion arises, to refer to some part of the course of instruction which he received inattentively months before. For such purposes a method of guidance to sources of information which would be under the control of the user would seem to be desirable. One such form of guidance might be comparable to the maps of municipal transportation systems, which, at the press of a button, illuminate the route between two points. Another form might be based upon the programmed learning machines. A feasibility study, at least, should be made.

PROGRAM 16. IMPROVEMENT OF METHODS
FOR NOTE-TAKING AND COPYING

It is unnecessary to emphasize the importance of copying devices in libraries, both to their users and to the libraries themselves. Each advance in the copying art has been avidly appropriated by libraries.

Present developments in office copying equipment make it possible for a library to provide adequate full-scale copies of textual material, without laboratory processing, at prices of from 10¢ to 25¢ per page. These processes are still not wholly adequate for library work. While further improvement may be expected, it is unlikely that the per-page cost of copying by these processes will be reduced in the foreseeable future to the point where they can meet the needs of scholarly photocopying. The following devices are, in consequence, still needed:

a. A device to make it possible for an inquirer to copy extracts (portions of pages) at full scale from bound volumes. Such a device should (1) be inexpensive in both original and operating cost and (2) portable; (3) should show results immediately without laboratory processing; and (4) should have good characteristics of resolution and ability to reproduce continuous tone.

b. A device to make it possible for an individual inquirer to copy full pages from bound volumes, realizing the savings in cost and space to be gained from use of microphotography at a 5- to 20-diameter reduction. Such a device should have characteristics similar to those of the extract-copying device.

c. A device to make it possible for an individual inquirer to make use of microcopies at a 5- to 20-diameter reduction. Such a device should be (1) inexpensive, (2) portable, and (3) convenient to use.

The development of such devices may be expected very greatly to facilitate the scholarly accumulation of research data as well as to liberate to home and private office use the exploitation of microtext which is now restricted by the necessity for viewing it on costly institutionalized equipment and by the necessity of securing expensive re-enlargements of individual pages.

None of these devices come within the scope of commercial interest and their development for library work must consequently be subsidized. Although attempts at the development of such devices have been proceeding

for many years,[17] their lack of success to date must not
be allowed to discourage still further efforts.

PROGRAM 17. STUDIES FOR IMPROVED BUILDING DESIGN

There is little that can be called scientific in the development of library architecture. New buildings do, of
course, reflect the experience — the mature experience
— of architects, librarians, and building committees,
but this experience is for the most part almost entirely
qualitative and rule-of-thumb in character and rarely
represents the testing of specific alternatives or hypoth-
eses. For example, librarians are anxious to secure buildings requiring the least amount of supervision, but the
means by which this can be best obtained have not been
experimentally ascertained. The same is true of the
rules by which (in educational institutions) the ratio of
seating capacity to student body is reached. The relation
of architecture to rate of delivery of books from the book
stacks has been mentioned in Program 9. Other matters
which call for formal inquiry are the matter of exits, control, illumination, departmentation, overflow storage facilities, etc.

The research library is called upon to meet a greater
diversity of needs than almost any other building, since
it must typically serve the layman and the expert, the

....
[17] J. Stewart and others, *Reading Devices for Micro-Images*
(*State of the Library Art,* vol. 5, part 2) (New Brunswick, N.J.:
Graduate School of Library Service, Rutgers University, 1960);
V. W. Clapp, "In Quest of an Optical Grail: The Search for an
Inexpensive Hand-Reader for Microtext," *ALA Bulletin* 55:
154-157 (February, 1961).

undergraduate and the professor, the generalist and the specialist. Its planning can contribute greatly either to the satisfaction or to the frustration of the needs for which it is frequented. A program of needed research should be laid out and followed.

PROGRAM 18. STANDARDIZATION AND TESTING OF LIBRARY EQUIPMENT, SUPPLIES, AND SYSTEMS

The Library Technology Project of the American Library Association was established in May, 1959, to undertake programs for testing, standardization, and development of library supplies, equipment, and systems, and for conveying information on these topics to librarians.

The project issues an *Annual Report* recording its activities. It prepares a column for publication in the *ALA Bulletin* and *Special Libraries* and issues a series of publications in which are reported the results of its major projects.

It provides a reference service by mail and telephone on library equipment and supplies; it has prepared a number of leaflets on subjects of particular interest; and it has distributed to libraries a number of publications containing purchasing information. It presents exhibits at library conferences and organized in 1962 a special Library Equipment Institute. It sponsors Sectional Committee Z-85 (library equipment and supplies) of the American Standards Association, representing both the consumers and the manufacturers of such goods, with a number of subcommittees on principal categories of equipment and supplies.

Among the topics investigated and reported or currently under investigation by the project (typically through testing, investigative, or developmental contracts) are the following (* = report published):

Adhesives*
Book-charging system for small libraries
Book-labeling device
Catalog card stock*
Equipment for photocopying from bound volumes*
Equipment for producing full-scale copies from micro-text*
Equipment for testing wood furniture
Improved adhesive for labeling books
Improved archival container
Improved fire insurance protection for libraries*
Improved newspaper stick
Improved package for shipping books
Improved pamphlet box
Ink for marking manuscripts*
Library-type record players*
Manual on floors and floor coverings
Manual on library furniture
Microfilm finder-reader system
Mylar laminating equipment*
Performance standards for library bookbinding*
Pressure-sensitive tapes
Protective coatings for microfilm
Reproduction of catalog cards
State-of-the art report on microfiches
Systems for circulation control*

The mere recital of this list of topics is evidence both

of the wide variety of technological information and development needed in these days for the support of library work, and also of the highly technical nature of much of the investigation required.

The program has hitherto been supported by grant funds. It is unlikely that such support can be expected indefinitely at the level at which it has been available since 1959. Because library work is likely to become more rather than less dependent upon technological applications, and is consequently likely to have increasing rather than less need for testing, standardizing, and developmental facilities, it seems requisite that other sources of support be found for this work than those now available. It has been suggested that the American Library Association might provide testing and developmental services under contract to state and other library agencies. In any case, ways for continuing this important program should be pursued.

PROGRAM 19. DEVELOPMENT OF NEW OR IMPROVED DEVICES FOR LIBRARY APPLICATIONS

All library work is dependent upon devices. The seeming simplicity of the library catalog card conceals the fact that this is one of the most flexible and versatile devices ever applied to bibliographical and library work. But to take advantage of this versatility, other and much more complicated devices — typewriters, duplicating and printing machines, cameras, punched-card handling systems, etc. — have become involved.

A number of needed devices mentioned in the programs previously described are included with others in the following list.

Copying

A portable device for rapid, dry, inexpensive, full-scale copying of extracts from books (Program 16).

Microcopying

Devices for making, storing, retrieving, viewing, and re-enlarging microcopies at high reduction (e.g., 200 diameters) (Program 1).

A scholar's camera for making rapid, dry, inexpensive microcopies at reductions of 5 to 20 diameters (Program 16).

A convenient, inexpensive hand reader for individual viewing of microcopies at a 5- to 20-diameter reduction (Program 16).

Catalog card production

A catalog card typewriter platen.

A hopper to feed catalog cards into a typewriter.

A "cataloger's camera" or other card-duplicating device for producing complete catalog card sets (main entry plus filing entries) at one action.

Production of catalogs in book format

An improved card-shingling device.

A variable aperture camera.

Other devices for rapid and inexpensive preparation of reproduction copy for book-format catalogs from stored information (e.g., on printed or punched cards, punched tape, or computer tape).

Telefacsimile

Devices for rendering telefacsimile adequate in speed, cost, and quality of output for library applications.

Computer applications

To descriptive cataloging.

To subject cataloging and indexing.

To serial records (Program 13).

To information storage and retrieval, including preparation of bibliographies.

To acquisitions searching (Program 12).

To circulation control (Program 14).

To catalog maintenance, including maintenance of union catalogs and lists and production of book-format catalogs (Program 3).

Bookbinding and preparation

Improved adhesives for "perfect" binding for libraries (Program 7).

Improved adhesives for labeling.

Book-label imprinter for both single and multiple label production.

Smythe-type sewing machine for library binding (Program 7).

Storage and service

Improved book-conveying equipment (Program 9).

Nonslip bookends.

Improved devices for recording location of books not on shelf, including those charged out of the building (Program 14).

Devices for detecting pilferage (Program 11).

Improved book bin (nonpilferable; also nondamaging to books).

Guidance to readers

Devices for guiding readers to appropriate sources of information (Program 15).

Miscellaneous
Devices for making random filing possible.
Devices for work-simplification.
Improved catalog card trays.
The above list could be extended. It is, however, sufficient to illustrate the need for new and improved technical devices for library work. It may be hoped that some of these devices will come into being through commercial enterprise, although this is unfortunately not frequently the case because of the smallness of the library market. Others may similarly be developed by individual libraries or by organizations such as the Library Technology Project, discussed under Program 18. In any event, it is desirable that continuous pressure be exerted, whether by associations of librarians or other agencies, to equip libraries with the tools that they need.

PROGRAM 20. IMPROVEMENT OF ORGANIZATION
OF LIBRARY SERVICES

Due to a number of circumstances, the original service boundaries for which many reference and research libraries were designed have broken down, with major resultant problems. It has become apparent that the hitherto prevailing pattern of organization of such service is in many respects no longer capable of meeting the need.
The principal factors contributing to this situation are the rapid extension of the single-jurisdiction muncipality into the multiple-jurisdiction metropolitan area, together with the general greatly increased need for and

dependence upon reference and research library resources.

Simultaneously with industry's spread beyond the city limits it has acquired an increasing need for the library service which it left behind and to which it no longer contributes tax support. The same is true of many suburban communities which lack adequate reference library facilities of their own and look to the metropolitan centers to which they are culturally but not jurisdictionally attached. As a result, municipal libraries find themselves deluged with requests from outside the taxing area, while their adult readers are crowded from their reading rooms by students who for a variety of reasons find it impossible or inconvenient to use the libraries of their own institutions.

Meanwhile, too, industry and industrial research tend to congregate in the vicinity of colleges and universities, attracted in part by the prospect of using the library facilities there. The situation in which libraries find themselves more and more under pressure from groups for whose service they were not originally planned has recently been identified by a president of the American Library Association as the number one library problem.[18]

On the scale of the metropolitan area, in consequence, it is increasingly apparent that reference and research library services must be replanned in the light of the realities of need and tax support. The same is true on the regional scale (e.g., that of a state). The demand for reference and research library materials by business,

. . . .

[18] J. E. Bryan, "Students, Libraries and the Educational Process," *ALA Bulletin* 56:707-715 (September, 1962).

industry, the professions, and education continues to increase. If maximum advantage is to be gained from the resources of the region, and if unnecessary duplication is to be avoided, the situation requires that in addition to local library services proportioned to local needs and capabilities, there be organization of the reference and research library resources of the region so to make them available, to the fullest extent, to all within the region.

There are obvious difficulties in reaching this objective. The first of these consists in the property rights and local responsibilities of owning institutions, due to the fact that they are typically organized and supported to serve specific local clienteles. Another is the difficulty of ascertaining where materials are located and of developing the mechanisms for sharing the use of them.

A number of approaches are being made to both problems. These include the search for methods by which to overcome local jurisdictional and institutional boundaries in the provision of library service. At the regional level a number of efforts are aimed at developing statewide sharing of resources through payments to individual libraries possessing strong collections in return for extension of their services.[19] A number of university libraries have instituted fee systems covering service to industrial

. . . .

[19] For example: L. A. Martin and others, *Library Service in Pennsylvania, Present and Proposed. A Survey Commissioned by the Pennsylvania State Librarian* . . . (Harrisburg: State Library, 1958); New York State Education Department, *Knowledge Is Power. Organizing Research of Yesterday and Today for Use Today and Tomorrow. The Regents [sic] Proposals* . . . (Albany: The University of the State of New York, The State Education Department, revised 1962).

and other private groups in their areas,[20] although none as yet appear to have developed special services to such groups as have been in effect for nearly fifteen years by a principal privately endowed reference library.[21]

In one state there has been a formal inquiry into the methods by which the services of university, school, and local public libraries may be coordinated in the interest especially of service to students.[22]

Much study, experiment, demonstration, and legislation will be required before these problems can be resolved. It is possible at the present time to suggest the topics for some of these:

Development of improved techniques for providing union catalog or alternative sources of information regarding the library resources of an area to persons within the area.

Development and demonstration of arrangements for sharing library services across taxing area boundaries.

Demonstration of library service to industry in multijurisdictional metropolitan areas.

Demonstration of effective library service to students.

. . . .

[20] "Stanford University Curtails Library Privileges to Non-University Readers," *Library Journal* 87:1438 (April 1, 1962); "The Relationship of Academic Libraries to the Off-Campus Research Community," papers by James C. Andrews, Robert Muller, David Weber, *in* Association of Research Libraries, *Minutes* 62:8-38 (July 13, 1963).

[21] H. H. Henkle, "Crerar's Research Information Service Explained," *Library Journal* 74:93-96 (January 15, 1949).

[22] J. A. Humphry, *Library Cooperation. The Brown University Study of University-School-Community Library Coordination in the State of Rhode Island* (Providence: Brown University Press, 1963).

Exploration of the appropriate role of the university in providing library services to industry and other non-university research.

PROGRAM 21. RECRUITMENT AND TRAINING
FOR LIBRARY WORK

From the over-all point of view, the problems of recruitment and training for library work may be summed up in one phrase — the scarcity of qualified personnel.

The rapid growth of library work would alone account in considerable part for this scarcity. A number of contributing causes can, however, be identified.

a. *The impossibility of providing trained personnel for all positions.*

While the basic requirements for the practice of law or medicine are identical no matter where the art is to be practiced, only a small part of their training will be identical for librarians who are severally to supervise a school library, serve as custodian of manuscripts in a library for medieval studies, perform reference work in a large law library, or serve in a pharmaceutical documentation center using a computer.

Library schools, given but one year to prepare college and university graduates for library work, necessarily attempt to provide the "core" training constituting the common denominator of preparation for the work. Although they also provide some specialist courses in bibliography and administration preparatory for service in medical, law, children's, and other specialized libraries, yet they obviously cannot create paleographers, lawyers, physicists, or Orientalists. In any case, the demand for such specialists is very occasional compared with that for public library service. As a result, it is common practice to recruit specialist librarians from the ranks of the subject disciplines, hoping that they will pick up the necessary knowledge of library work on the job; and this is most likely to be true if the appointing authority is not aware of or actually disparages the value of library training. Many mistakes have been made as a result.

b. *The economic aspects.*

Library salary scales tend to lag behind those of other employments. There is little to persuade a graduate with a major in chemistry or an engineering degree to spend another year in school in order to become a librarian, if he can secure the same or larger income immediately as a chemist or engineer.

Furthermore, although there are copious sources of assistance for graduate work in other lines of endeavor, there are few sources of fellowships and scholarships for the fifth year of university attendance required for training in library work, which in consequence loses in the competition for graduates.

c. *Other factors.*

Among other contributing causes may be mentioned the difficulty of conveying to potential recruits an adequate understanding of the realities of library work, so much of which is behind the scenes, while what is on view frequently holds little challenge. There is also the reluctance of marriageable young women to work in institutions where there is a dearth of marriageable young men, and the corresponding reluctance of men to get into work that has become marked as women's. Still another cause may lie in the inefficient use of professional manpower and the dilution of professional assignments in many libraries with subprofessional and clerical tasks.

The problems of recruitment and training for library work have had the continuous attention of the professional library associations since their beginnings in the last quarter of the nineteenth century; and the intervening period has been punctuated by a number of notable special studies and reports. At the present time several of the associations in the United States have scholarship or fellowship funds; while the American Library Association not only maintains a special Office for Recruitment but has established as well a Commission on a National Plan for Education in Librarianship.

It is to be hoped that from the investigations and deliberations of the last-named body may emerge recommendations upon which may be based a program directed at meeting at least some of the problem situations identified above.

INDEX